British-Israel

Fact *not Fiction*

A Rudimentary Guide
for
Students of the subject

by

Major-General C. A. Hadfield

THE COVENANT PUBLISHING CO. LTD.

2015

First Edition 1920
Third Edition 1926
Fourth Edition, revised and reprinted 2015

ISBN 978-085205-103-0

Printed by
THE COVENANT PUBLISHING COMPANY LIMITED
121, Low Etherley, Bishop Auckland,
Co. Durham, DL14 0HA
www.covpub.co.uk

-

FOREWORD

BY

THE RIGHT REV. THE

LORD BISHOP OF THE FALKLAND ISLANDS

Having been asked by Major-General C. A. Hadfield to write a short preface to the book which he is now presenting to the public, I do so with the greatest pleasure.

The book is exactly what is needed.

The subject of which it treats is of the highest importance, and it is the intention of the writer to try and place in the hands of busy people a little introduction to this great subject which can be easily read and digested, and which may awaken a desire for further study.

Nothing could have been better done. The writer begins by drawing attention to the distinction between Israel and Judah; it is very simple, but so many people fail to grasp that very elementary fact.

All Jews are Israelites; but all Israelites are not Jews! All Yorkshiremen are Englishmen; but all Englishmen are not Yorkshiremen!

As Yorkshire is a county in England, so Judah is a county in Israel.

The "Whole House of Israel" is used as referring to both Israel (the North) and Judah (the South); but the title "Israel" is never used of Judah alone. Judah, of course, being the Jews. There is another point well worked out, viz., the certainty of the working out of the prophecies concerning Israel. If the British Empire is not Israel, then none of the prophecies concerning Israel are YET fulfilled.

Then we are on the horns of a dilemma; first, God has failed in His promise; secondly: we shall lose all we have got, and God has been playing with us, for WE hold all that Israel is supposed to hold, and yet there is some other nation not yet developed which is to take all this, as well as our unique character and reputation in the world (for Israel is to have it)—and if we are not Israel, we shall have to give it all up, and even the Coronation stone itself.

All these points are carefully worked out, and yet in such a way that it can be easily understood.

I should like to add that General Hadfield has confined himself to the tracing of the Identity.

So many exponents of this great fact have added theories of their own, going into all sorts of side issues, and even identifying the Kaiser and the German war, in the prophecies. These things do more harm than good. What we are concerned with is: "Does Israel, as distinct from the Jews, exist?" If so, does Great Britain in any way correspond to the description of Israel in the latter days?

The readers of this book will answer these questions, and, I feel sure, that if they take up the study with an open mind they cannot fail to decide in favour of what many of us hold to be the vindication of the truth of God as set forth in the Prophets.

The rock on which so many split is the very same as led the Chief Priests, Scribes, and Pharisees astray in our Lord's Day.

Because He did not come according to their preconceived ideas, and because they did not interpret the Prophets as God intended them to be received, as in many ways a literal statement of the approach of the Coming one, such Messianic chapters as Isaiah 53 were actually overlooked.

As they rejected Him, so many reject the literal foreshadowing of Israel's (the Northern Kingdom) future in the "latter days," and say that God has taken these promises from Israel and given them to another, preserving the Tribe of Judah, which none can deny; although Israel had nothing to do with the Crucifixion of Christ.

4

That God should deny Himself is far harder to believe than that He is carrying out only His Written Word by means of His Own People, to whom Great Britain so closely corresponds.

I therefore commend this book to all, and I trust that the Blessing of God may rest upon it.

N. S. FALKLAND ISLES

October, 1920

SECOND FOREWORD

General Hadfield has kindly sent me the additions he has made to the Second Edition of "British-Israel, Facts Not Fancies."* I am delighted there is to be a Second Edition.

I fully agree with the improvements he has made, and again I pray that this book may be prospered and I shall look forward to the production of a Third Edition.

N. S. FALKLAND ISLES

Valparaiso

*Note: title change for the Fourth Edition

CONTENTS

AUTHOR'S NOTE

Always in reading Holy Scripture realise that—

For the reader to understand the great distinction between the term "Israel," and the term "Judah"—or "the Jews," it must be *thoroughly understood* that "Israel" refers to the Ten Tribed Northern Kingdom of Samaria which went into ASSYRIAN Captivity, and *never returned to Palestine.* The Jews are those who (much later) went into BABYLONIAN Captivity, and who, 70 years later, returned with the tribe of Benjamin and a portion of Levi. See *Matthew* 10:5-7; *Jeremiah* 3:14 and 18; *Amos* 9:9; *Hosea* 9:17; *Jeremiah* 31:10; 23:1-6.

Jesus said: "The Scriptures must be Fulfilled" (*Mark* 14:49)

INTRODUCTION

"THY WORD IS TRUE FROM THE BEGINNING" (*Psalm* 119:160)

In considering the question whether or not a literal Israel (other than those known as the "Jews") exists to-day, we must face the fact that "the Scriptures were written for our learning," and that they contain certain "signs" for our guidance and help. Take for example *Hosea* 12:1, "Ephraim ... followeth after the East wind." This expression shows us that Ephraim-Israel was predestined to move (i.e., from Assyrian captivity) in a Westerly direction.

The mention here of "Ephraim" also denotes for our guidance, that the passage does not refer to the race known to us as "The Jews": they being descendants of Judah, whereas Ephraim is of Joseph's stock: quite a distinct race, and we know *"the Birthright"* was Joseph's not Judah's (I *Chronicles* 5:1).

Therefore if Ephraim-Israel moved from Assyria to the "Isles of the West"—the text is fulfilled; and we have proof of an Israel journeying Westward to the "place appointed"—of which more anon. Then, as regards an "Everlasting Throne," and it *must* be so, because God has told us in the Bible that the throne of David was established *for ever*: hence, unless we are going so far as to doubt God's Word, we must believe that the "Throne of David" is still, to this day, in existence. (See *Psalm* 89:3-4).

Did not our Lord also tell us that He came "to redeem the promises made to the fathers"? i.e., That Israel (apart from the Jews) should be an "Everlasting Nation," sent to an "appointed place," and for safe dwelling? And do not the Prophets reveal that the "appointed place" denotes an Island home?

No wonder many are "blind," when we consider the Words of Christ—"O fools and slow of heart to believe *all* that the prophets have spoken" (*Luke* 24:25). And then, in the additional remark, "And beginning at Moses and *all* the prophets He expounded unto them in all the Scriptures the things concerning Himself."

Remember—the only "Scriptures" of Our Lord's day was the Old Testament.

God's plan was not to destroy Israel but rather to conceal the Hebrews—other than the Jews—and guard and guide them to a new country, speaking a new language, and bearing a new name.

Abraham Lincoln said: "The man who will not investigate both sides of a question is dishonest."

The following notes of a rudimentary character are put together in the hope of their being helpful to those who are confused in distinguishing between the term Israel and the term Jew; and to assist them in coming to an understanding as to what is meant by "British-Israel."

Although the history of Israel—as a nation—ceases in the Old Testament, after the Northern Kingdom—who were known as the "Ten-Tribed House," were exiled to captivity in Assyria—yet the Bible assures us that Israel as "a Nation" *will exist for ever,* so we know that "the Nation" did not become extinct, but that it was God's Divine plan, that under *the name* of Israel the Northern Kingdom should disappear both in the Bible and in history—*but only in name.* (See Chap. XV).

We have also many "signs" to guide us that Israel, under a new name, and speaking a new language, would arise, with a great destiny to play in the world's history.

The following notes are to show how clear it is that Israel—as apart from the Jews—the Fifth or "Stone Kingdom" (of Daniel) and the British race—or the English-speaking races—are all identical! A living literal Israel, thus making the Old Testament History clear and intelligible, and a sound argument with which to confound all infidels, agnostics, and scoffers, who are eager to claim that God's promises on oath to Abraham and his seed have never been fulfilled. They have been, and *are being* fulfilled to the very letter! "Despise not prophesying" (II *Thessalonians* 5:20). There are many good and earnest Bible students who have been from their infancy taught—and, unfortunately, are still being taught—that the *only* Israel we know on this earth is the Jews.

Then, again, how many Bible students are there who are unable to grasp the "past," the "present," and the "future" history of Israel.

At one time God forsook Israel, but He immediately after promised mercy and forgiveness to poor sinful Israel. When they were prepared to forsake idols, they were to become "Sons of the living God," i.e., Christians. Then, finally, the Israelites and the Jews will *all* be known and recognised; and, as prophesied, will be rejoined under one head as related in *Hosea* 1. That day is surely at hand—look at events in the world. This must be prior to the Millennium, for Israel *now* holds the Sceptre of Judah.

There is a Divine purpose in blinding the eyes of the world generally to a living literal Israel. That "blindness" is passing away—the eyes are gradually being opened—"The Scriptures cannot be broken" (*John* 10:35).

May the day be not far distant when the eyes of our Church leaders will be opened to the need of a revision being made in the headings at the top of the chapters of the Old Testament. They are misleading, for it is quite impossible for "the Church" to accept all the promises made to Israel. The error arose with the ancient commentators, but the perpetuity of such errors in these days, when history has taught us much, is a mistake—nay, disastrous.

When will the British remember that God said: "Ye are My witnesses, and My servant whom I have chosen" (*Isaiah* 43:10).

Who does this refer to, if not to the British race?

We British as a race are woefully and wilfully ignorant of our origin, and of our national heritage and ancestry from

"Ephraim-Israel."

Probably this ignorance has been ordained by Divine Will in order to carry out God's plan for Israel to pass through the centuries *unrecognised* as such.

Now that we approach the "last days" of the Christian era the imposed "ignorance" is being gradually lifted, and much of what has been a "sealed book" is opened. "The eyes of the blind shall be opened" we read, therefore, if we will not take our opportunity of enquiring into our national ancestry we are wilfully blind! We are given certain "signs" to guide us. Look at the part and position the Anglo-Saxon race take in the world and in the very life of Mankind! Who are the English? Why is it that to the Anglo-Saxon people the Bible takes so prominent a place—and is, by them, so widely distributed throughout the heathen world? Is it not because of its racial heritage from Israel to Israel in perpetuity? How is it that the Anglo-Saxons so wonderfully fulfil all the characteristics laid down for Israel? The only answer is that it is proof that God has kept, is keeping, and will keep, all His promises. He further promised that he would appoint a place (i.e., other than Palestine) "for My people Israel," and He promised that the separated House of Judah should walk with (or as in the margin *to*) the House of Israel for a reunion of the twelve tribes.

It is impossible for anyone, however much he may argue, to prove from God's Word that "The Church" replaced a living literal Israel, which upon God's oath, was to be an "everlasting Nation," and, in the "last days," was preordained to possess certain fully enumerated characteristics and to occupy certain parts of the Earth.

True the bulk of church-goers accept this vague teaching, but only because they have accepted it from their youth up. It will not bear the test of investigation, and therefore is answerable for much of the confusion in the minds of scholars, critics and Bible students generally; as it is, for much of the unbelief in the Bible. These good people cannot, in reading the Old Testament, manage to "square" the promise of Israel and Judah reuniting because, like the ancient commentators of the early centuries, they know no other Israel than the Jews.

Those who read the Old Testament as meaning what the written words express, can clearly see a foretold history of an Israel speaking another language than Hebrew—as promised by God. So to them the truth of the Prophets and the inspiration of the Bible are assured.

For this sole reason the study of the subject is valuable because it satisfies students in all respect that the English-speaking races of to-day are the actual descendants of the so-called "Lost Ten Tribes"; and moreover are the "Stone Kingdom" of the Book of *Daniel*. This proof is sufficient to prevent anyone from becoming an unbeliever, a Higher Critic, or an Agnostic, which is quite a sufficient reply to those who immediately ask: "Well, even if your view is correct, what is the good of being a British-Israelite?"

*   *   *   *

Our knowledge of early British history is limited, and many are too apt to be satisfied by commencing with the Caesars. Why commence so late? Why imagine our national history only started from Rome? Green's *History of the English People* says: "For the fatherland of the English race we must look far away from England itself"—and the historian goes on to locate it in Northern Europe, but he does not go back beyond the fifth century, where he finds them as Angles, Jutes, Saxons, etc. The Israelites, as has been shown, when they left their Assyrian Captivity made their way to the Southern shore of the Caspian Sea and thence on into Central and Northern Europe.

Is it not safe to accept the Bible as being, not only our Manual of Religion, but our Manual of History? That it gives us the foretold history of an ever-living Israel—"the Everlasting Nation"? Why, for instance, were the Romans unable to remain in the British Isles?

Because, centuries before, the everlasting throne of David had, for its safety and security, been transferred from Palestine to the British Isles, and no weapon which was formed was to destroy it or to prosper. Our national archives denote from the recorded charts, how our Royal House is directly descended from the House of David.

Thus it was God's plan of preserving Israel in safety—and *unrecognised.*

The utterances of some of our public men, made probably in ignorance or unbelief of any connection in their minds of Israel being existent in the British race are of themselves remarkable. The late Mr. Joseph Chamberlain, for example, once publicly said: "The British race is a race specially chosen for a specific purpose in the world with great responsibilities."

Then again the present Archbishop of Canterbury in a sermon remarked: "Do we constantly realise that we alone to-day are those whom God hath chosen in the world's history as a people to whom is to be given incomparably the greatest trust and decision for the world's safety that has ever been laid upon a great company of people?"

Our learned men are profoundly ignorant of the early history of our race. More knowledge of the history of the Saxons, Goths, Dacians, and Asiatic Scythians is needed. But in consequence of this "ignorance" it has been possible for Israel to exist and without the envy of other races to rise to the preordained greatness which was destined so long ago for "Israel" to possess in the "last days."

God's plan was to sow and scatter Israel through the "seven times" period of punishment. It was not until after the Reformation that Israel was allowed to "settle down" and make their influence felt in distant lands. Their "Mission" was then to commence, their task, which was to build up the Empire—of "The Stone Kingdom"—to its future greatness as a Nation and a Company of Nations, i.e., as a Commonwealth of "free," not "subject" States, free to stay in, or leave the Empire as they willed.

That they will remain as a part thereof is a foregone conclusion! Our national history is a history which we may say our modern historians have failed to satisfactorily solve, arranged probably again, in order to complete God's plan of concealment of Israel *until* "*the appointed time*" when their existence shall be made generally known. Sharon Turner went so far as to locate the Saxons in Central Asia, from whence he traces them to the British Isles. If, as he says, they lived to the east of Araxe, we get to the very locality to which Israel had been carried captive, which is significant.

Where the Historian pauses let us now refer to the Old Testament giving us the history of Israel and may we say the early history foretold of the Anglo-Saxons. See II *Kings* 17:6: "In the ninth year of Hoshea, the King of Assyria took Samaria and carried Israel away into Assyria and placed them in Halah and in Habor by the river of Gozan and in the Cities of the Medes." (This was about 725 BC).

Why should we resent what seems to be so reasonably clear proof of our ancestry? Why should we resent the idea of our race springing directly from Abraham? It was through Isaac, i.e., "by faith" that God brought Abraham into the land of Canaan from the other side of the river Euphrates. See *Joshua* 24:3, "And I took your father Abraham from the other side of the flood ..." The Hebrew word here for "flood" is NAHAR, which means "a river" (doubtless the Euphrates in this reference). From Abraham came *three* distinct races.

1. The Ishmaelites from Hagar, i.e., The Ishmaelites—or Arabs.
2. The race from Keturah—or the Indians and Japanese.
3. The race from Isaac and Jacob, or the Israelites and the Jews.

With this third distinct race we read in *Genesis* 27:21, "But my Covenant will I establish with Isaac." *Not with the other of Abraham's sons*—but with Isaac's Sons—Saxons with the 'I' changed! These, *only*, are the children and heirs of the Covenants and promises to Abraham. We are told much about Abraham, his name signifies, Ab—father, Ra—great, Ham—multitude. God sent away the sons of the concubines of Abraham. They went eastward. Where are their descendants? They must be among the living races of the world, just as much as are the Jews from the son Judah.

Anyone who desires to study this subject is referred to the writings of the Rev. Joseph Wild DD, which are most interesting.

It is amusing to hear educated persons talking of Abraham being "a Jew," and of God bringing "the Jews" out of Egypt, and so on!

Abraham was a Hebrew—but how could he possibly be "a Jew"? The first mention of the Jews was centuries after Abraham's day. (See II *Kings* 16:6).

*　　*　　*　　*

To arrive at the origin of the word BRITISH. It began as BRITH, or Covenant, made between GOD, and Abraham and his wife Sarah. The Hebrew word Brith (Covenant) and ISH (man) makes up our word BRITISH; and the entry into the "Isles of the West," or the "United Kingdom," in the early days BC, constitutes the origin of the British Colony.

These notes go on to show how Zedekiah was the last of the line of David to occupy the Throne of David in Judah. That the King's daughter went thenceforth to Egypt in charge of the Prophet Jeremiah, and from there to Ireland, where the throne was established over the House of Israel—*to this day.*

Remember always that although the Old Testament does not disclose the final movements of Zedekiah's daughter and the Prophet Jeremiah, it emphatically records:

1. The Throne of David shall be "everlasting."
2. There shall be an "appointed place" (i.e., other than Palestine) for "My people Israel" (i.e., other than the Jews).
3. The reunion of the twelve tribes.

4. Israel to possess all its heritages "from the River in Egypt to the Great River Euphrates."

So we may well consider those words: "If ye believe not the prophets, neither will ye believe though one rose from the dead."

Have we all realised that if—as God's Word tells us—the "Sceptre should not depart from Judah" ... "until Shiloh came"... that if "a sceptre" means a King—there must be "a Kingdom"? Therefore if Shiloh refers to Christ "the Kingdom" (of Israel) must exist until our Saviour's "Second Coming" and "Israel" holds that Kingdom and performs Christ's Missionary work *now* (to the extent of nearly ninety per cent of the world). Therefore Israel is a great, powerful, and wealthy Nation. The "Chief of Nations," in fact, for none other could accomplish the work! Where then is Israel?

The human race is composed of Israel, and Gentiles; but to reckon the English speaking races as "Gentiles" is to confuse the whole of the prophetical writings forecasting the world destiny of God's Israelitish people whose kingdom was to be an everlasting one. There is as much confusion over the term Gentile as there is in distinguishing Israel from the race known as "The Jews."

As regards the fallacy that "Israel" became "The Church." It is pointed out in the Reference Bible by the Rev. C. I. Scofield DD, that "Israel" in the Land is never called "a Church." In the Wilderness Israel was a true Church but not in any sense the N.T. Church (see *Acts* 7:38; *Hebrews* 12:23; *Matthew* 16:18). Both were "called out" by the same God, but this is the only similarity.

CHAPTER I

DISTINCTION BETWEEN ISRAEL AND THE JEWS

There are many people who seem quite unable to distinguish between the term "Israel" and the term "The Jews." They seem to imagine that the terms are synonymous; but the races are distinct and separate. The Jews are only descended from *one* of Jacob's twelve sons, and therefore can only comprise one-twelfth part of Israel. The Jews, or "The House of Judah," were originally known as the "Southern Kingdom." The Israelites are the descendants of ten of Jacob's sons, called "The House of Israel," and were originally known as the "Northern Kingdom." In stating this, we exclude the "House of Levi," for they had no inheritance, and were reserved for priestly offices, so do not count as a tribe. (*Numbers* 26:62; *Deuteronomy* 10:9; 18:2).

The Northern Kingdom are spoken of as "The lost Ten Tribes." This is because they were (in consequence of their evil ways) carried away into captivity by Shalmaneser, king of Assyria, as related in II *Kings* 17. The Old Testament does not further record the history of these ten tribes; but the Old Testament contains many "signs" by which we can be sure, that although the "Northern Kingdom" was to disappear under the *name* of Israel, they were to reappear under a *new* name, and speaking a *changed* language. Do we not read: "For with stammering lips, and another tongue will he speak to this people?" (*Isaiah* 28:11). The preceding verse 10 is another "sign" to us of the change of language. And then we read: "And thou shalt be called by a new name, which the mouth of the Lord shall name (*Isaiah* 62:2); "... And call His Servants by another name" (*Isaiah* 65:15). Thus we have God's word as a warning that it is useless for us to look for Israel as a nation under that name, or speaking a Hebrew tongue. Both name and language, we are told in Holy Scripture, were to be *changed.* (See Chap. XV).

From the time of exile the name Israel disappears as a nation, not so the Jews. Some 133 years after the exile of Israel (which took place as regards the main body 721 BC) the House of Judah, accompanied by the Tribe of Benjamin (temporarily detached from the Northern Kingdom) were also deported but by King Nebuchadnezzar to Babylon for a named period of seventy years (*Jeremiah* 25:11). At the end of that period the House of Judah (called the Jews), accompanied by the tribe of Benjamin (as representatives of the "House of Israel"), returned to Palestine (see *Ezra* 2). These tribes *alone* were in Palestine during our Lord's time on earth. And, with the exception of Judas Iscariot, who was a Jew (of Kerioth, in Judea), we can safely assume the Apostles were of the tribe of Benjamin, and therefore "Israelites," in contradistinction to "Jews." But in regard to "the race" of the Disciples see the further remarks in Chap. XVI.

"Israel" was the name given to Jacob, and to his twelve sons. It embraces the name: "The House of Israel," and "The House of Judah." It was, however, the name *especially reserved* for the "Northern Kingdom."

Thus the "House of Judah" is "of" Israel, from being descended from Jacob's son Judah; but cannot be styled "Israel."

There is absolutely no doubt about the *distinction* between Jew and Israelite; the Bible is clear and definite on this point, and if there be any confusion, it is solely in man's mind. There is no confusion in the Bible, as any readers can see for themselves by reference to the following passages, amongst others: I *Samuel* 11:8; II *Kings* 22:27; I *Chronicles* 28:4-5; II *Chronicles* 13:15-16; 15:9; 31:1; *Isaiah* 7:1-8, 17; 8:14; 10:12-13; 48:1; *Jeremiah* 3:8-18; 7:2-15; 11:10-17; 13:11; 31:31; 32:30-32; 33:14; 50:4-33; *Ezekiel* 23:4; 37:16-19; *Daniel* 9:7; *Hosea* 1:11; 4:15; 5:9, 15; 6:10-11; 8:14; 11:12; *Amos* 1:1; *Micah* 1:5; *Zechariah* 8:13; 10:6; *Hebrews* 8:8, etc.

To enable Students to readily and clearly follow the separate histories of the Israelites and of the Jews they must carefully study II *Kings* 17:6-23, and I *Chronicles* 5:26, relating to Israel's exile to Assyria, at which time the tribe of Benjamin was (temporarily) attached, although belonging to Ten-Tribed Israel, to the House of Judah. They did *not accompany "Israel" into exile* to Assyria.

During the seventy years of exile and intercourse and social contact with another race, they naturally lost touch with their Hebrew language, and it is not surprising that in order to be understood on their return to Palestine it was necessary to employ interpreters. (*Nehemiah* 8:4-9).

This fact is an object lesson for many of us to-day who so constantly ask if Israel exists would they not speak Hebrew? And would they not follow Hebraic Customs?

If seventy years caused the Jews to change their language so as to need interpreters, it follows that Israel, after nearly 2,700 years would not speak Hebrew. Moreover, the Scriptures tell us that Israel would speak in another tongue. Naturally all customs would equally change.

The Benjamites were never, *racially*, Jews. When they all returned to Palestine they became socially known as, and locally termed "Jews." (See *Ezra* 4:12). For example, in the Book of *Esther* 2:5, we read of—"a certain Jew whose name was Mordecai ... a Benjamite." He was a Jew locally by "custom," but certainly not by "race." It is precisely the same as regards St Paul, who calls himself "a Jew of Tarsus"; but who explains that he is "an Israelite of the tribe of Benjamin." (*Romans* 11:1; *Philippians* 3:5). Thus we have Scriptural evidence to support the distinction which does not seem to be generally understood, and hence so much confusion.

The Rev. J. H. Allen, the prominent American writer upon this subject, says: "The fallacy which Biblical interpreters have fallen into is, because they failed to understand the genealogy of the two Kingdoms, two houses of Israel, a Northern and a Southern Kingdom, a ten-tribed Kingdom, and a Kingdom which was eventually composed of *three* tribes, *who are the only* Israelites in Biblical *history called Jews*." The two families which "the Lord has chosen—Israel and Judah, the birthright family, of which Joseph, Rachel's son, is racial head, and Judah—the Sceptre family, of which Judah, Leah's son, is the racial head. One House, Kingdom, or Nation, was ruled over by the Leah-Judah family, and the other Commonwealth was ruled over by the Rachel-Joseph family. So the House of Israel and the House of Judah were not the posterity of the same mother, and the law of heredity would most naturally leave its impress.

"Then, when we remember that Joseph married an Egyptian woman, and that his posterity were half Egyptian, we understand that the 'House of Joseph' would be still further removed in form and features from the Jewish people. Yet in hunting for the lost 'tribes'—the Birthright House—the common mistake is made of looking for Jewish form and features, as well as for a people who observe the rite of circumcision. But the facts are that the House of Israel, of Samaria, had ceased the practice of circumcision two centuries before they left Samaria. They were cast out of Samaria because of their idolatry, and worship of the two Golden Calves which Jeroboam set up."

*   *   *   *

It may not be inappropriate to repeat here the words of Professor Totten, of Yale University. "I cannot" (he writes) "state too strongly that the man who has not seen that Israel of the Scriptures is totally different from the Jewish people is yet in the very infancy, the mere alphabet, of Biblical study, and that to this day the meaning of seven-eighths of the Bible is shut to his understanding."

We are told clearly (I *Kings* 11; 12) that the Hebrews were finally divided into two nations (about 974 BC).

David had joined Judah and Israel and ruled over them, yet in II *Samuel* 5:4-5, Israel is mentioned as *separate* from Judah. "In Hebron he (David) reigned over Judah seven years and six months: and in Jerusalem he reigned thirty and three years over 'All Israel and Judah.'"

"The Rev. L. G. A. Roberts remarks anent the ignorance of the term 'Jews'—in comparison with Israel:

" 'I am sorry so many people seem to read their Bibles with prejudiced eyes or biased minds: they should be given to understand that the House of Israel went into Captivity to Assyria in 721 BC. About seven or eight years after this, Sennacherib came up against all the fenced Cities of Judah and took them. (II *Kings* 18:13). On his tablets he states he took 200,150 Captives from 46 Strong Cities: these he took to Assyria. Now Judah was not *begun* to be taken away until about 108 years after, to BABYLON, which is some considerable distance South of Assyria.

" 'The return from Babylon under Cyrus is stated in *Ezra* 1:5 to be, Judah and Benjamin (2:1). The term *all Israel* is simply that Benjamin *belonged* to ALL ISRAEL (a *designation of the Northern Kingdom*), for Benjamin was a tribe lent out of the Kingdom (of Israel) to David that he might have a light always in Jerusalem, since Jerusalem belonged to the tribe of Benjamin.

" 'The tribe of Benjamin remained faithful to Judah until the Crucifixion (*Zechariah* 11:14), when, as they had been forewarned by Our Lord to His Disciples, and previously by Jeremiah the Prophet (6:1) they escaped out of Jerusalem, as also did Our Lord to His Disciples. Some few Israelites may have come to Babylon, but *Ezekiel* 11:15-16, gives us to understand that the Captivity of Jechoniah mainly joined the Ten Tribes. *This tribe of Judah has, ever since, been separated from Israel (Deuteronomy 33:7) and will remain so as far as the Jew is concerned until they are united, as stated in Ezekiel 37:15-22 which has not yet been effected.' "*

God said "Ephraim is My First-born." (See *Jeremiah* 31:9). In the original the same word expresses "first-born" and "birthright." Ephraim was the son of Joseph, and in I *Chronicles* 5:1, 2, we are told "the birthright was Joseph's"—and again we read that this birthright devolved upon Ephraim and Manasseh.

This is the race predestined of God to be for everlasting, and *quite* distinct and apart from "the Jews." God said: "How shall I give thee up Ephraim?" Is it then likely He would have cast them off?

Ephraim's descendants were destined by God, as we read in the Bible, to become a "multitude" or "fulness" of Nations (or fulness of the Gentiles for it is equally translated).

As God's "promises" were to "Ephraim-Israel" it is impossible to reconcile them as now being inherited by "the Jews" of the House of Judah. It is arguing that God has "failed," thus breaking down the very foundations of our faith, which is a despairing thought for those who either have not, or cannot see by modern history how exactly God has guarded, and guided "Ephraim-Israel" from the wilds of Assyrian Captivity to "the appointed place."

The people of the British Empire and of the United States of America are not likely to realise nationally that they are Ephraim-Israel until Armageddon proves it.

CHAPTER II

ISRAEL TO BE CONCEALED AND UNRECOGNISED

The Jews, although sent into exile for a term of *seventy years,* were predestined to be always known and recognised; they had their part to play in the Crucifixion of Christ. They returned to Palestine to carry out the prophecies. The death of our Lord rests with the Jews, and not with the Ten-Tribed House of Israel, for the latter, although exiled to Assyria, and "lost," as regards their name, language, and connection with the Northern Kingdom of Israel, were destined to play a great part in the future of the world's history. To perform this destiny it was God's Will that they should pass through the world "hidden," i.e., *unidentified* in any way as Israel, until the time of the end.

II *ESDRAS*

We are permitted to know in II *Esdras* 13:40-45, that the Ten Tribes *escaped* from Assyrian captivity, as the last two verses of *Jeremiah* 46 imply they should do.

Many good Bible students seem to imagine that because the Old Testament ceases to record an historical sequence of Israel's doings—as with the Jews—that Israel became practically extinct; or, if not extinct, of so little importance as to be swallowed up among the nations, leaving only the Jews as representatives of Israel's race in the world's future. Such a view as this is entirely against Holy Scriptures; and, moreover, it immediately throws a doubt upon the ability of God to fulfil the promises which He so emphatically, upon oath, swore would be fulfilled "in the latter days." It is a very serious misinterpretation of Holy Scriptures, for where can any Bible Student point to any passage which admits of changing a *literal* Israel into "the Church," or a "Spiritual Israel"?

Some years ago the late Dr. Ryle, Bishop of Liverpool, warned the clergy of daring to "spiritualise" Israel, saying he could find no authority for changing from a *literal* rendering of the Prophetical Books of the Old Testament! What a pity that more of our clergy cannot see *their* errors. Later will be shown what is probably the reason for this "confusion" in their minds over the term Israel and Judah.

We know that if Israel (of the Ten Tribes) has failed to exist, the Holy Scriptures cannot be fulfilled! Such an argument is *impossible*; "Scripture is given by the inspiration of God" (II *Timothy* 3:16). See also II *Peter* 1:21; and *Luke* 1:70; and II *Thessalonians* 5:20; and *John* 10:35. These passages must satisfy the greatest sceptic, if he believes in the Bible at all!

Let us here quote the words of the writer of the Book of *Esdras*, for although the Apocrypha is not one of the inspired books, it must be accepted as the best of ancient history; and in tracing "Israel" it is incumbent upon us to study the Bible together with history. These are the words of Ezra:

"Those are the ten tribes which were carried away prisoners out of their own land, in the time of Osea the King, whom Salmanasar, the king of Assyria, led away captive; and he carried them over the waters, and so came they into another land. But they took this counsel among themselves that they would leave the multitude of the heathen, and go forth into a further country, where never mankind dwelt; that they might there keep their statutes, which they never kept in their own land. And they entered into Euphrates by the narrow passages of the river, for the Most High then shewed signs for them, and held still the flood till they were passed over. For through that country there was a great way to go, namely, of a year and a half, and the same region is called Arsareth."

This is surely definite and clear proof that the Ten Tribes did escape from Assyria, and after wandering for one and a half years found their way to Arsareth, which locality may be identified with South Russia as we know it to-day.

Thus we are permitted to know the place of locating the Israelite captives, and we find the modern historian tracing the British back to the same place, which is significant of the latter being the descendants of the former, i.e., one and the same people. It is surely remarkable proof and worthy of consideration.

JOSEPHUS

But we have the writings of the Jewish Historian, Josephus (AD 70-90) to help us, he records that the Ten Tribes never returned to Palestine. This is borne out by Jerome, and also by the Greek historian Herodotus, and others writing later; moreover, we have ample scriptural proof that the Ten Tribes never, as "tribes," returned to Palestine, though possibly some individuals may have done so.

We have some Scriptural proof in support of this belief, for we read in II *Chronicles* 30:6: "And he will return to the *remnant* of you that *are escaped* out of the hand of the Kings of Assyria." (See II *Kings* 29; I *Chronicles* 5:26).

Thus a "remnant" returned to Palestine (i.e., a remnant of ten-tribed Israel), probably this was fore-ordained in order that their descendants should become "the men of Galilee" of Our Lord's day, and from whom, with the Benjamites, Christ selected His Disciples (with the exception of Judas Iscariot the Jew).

These Galileans, although *locally* looked upon, and classed as "Jews," were in fact of quite a distinct race (of Israel). We read in the New Testament that Peter's speech (as a Galilean) betrayed him— and again: "Are not all these which speak Galileans"? While in connection with the Ascension: "Ye men of Galilee."

The speech, and other peculiarities here denote the differences between the races, although *all* probably were termed as Jews in the days of Christ on Earth.

Through the providence of God, "the men of Galilee" were doubtless specially located in Palestine for a Divine purpose so that

27

Christ's Command to "the lost sheep of the House of Israel" could be fulfilled. This was not to be carried out by the Jews. St Paul was sent to *the Children of Israel*, commencing the Missioning efforts which were to convey the Gospel to all parts of the world. Did not St Paul preach through all the Coasts of Judea, and in Galatia, addressing them as "Men and Brethren, Children of the Stock of Abraham"?

CHAPTER III

SUGGESTIONS FOR SCEPTICS REGARDING PROPHECY

It is difficult to follow the minds of the sceptics, for can they not see how many of the prophecies have been actually fulfilled? They believed only those that they have seen; their eyes are blinded as regards an historical sequence of events—purposely blinded, no doubt. It is not their fault; for, in order that Israel might go forward to her great destiny in the world, it was, for Divine reasons, necessary that the eyes of the theologians, commentators, and teachers generally, should be "blinded" to the fact that any part of Israel other than the Jews, existed in the world.

⁓ Let us consider how many of the prophecies have been fulfilled. And, if so with these, why should we doubt any? With regard to our Lord we can read that—

Moses declared His family.

Micah	"	His place of birth.
Isaiah	"	The virginity of His Mother.
Zechariah	"	His triumphant entry into Jerusalem.
David	"	His Life, Resurrection, and Ascension.

Do not let us, with all the "signs" at hand for our guidance; and with the knowledge that so much, as originally prophesied, has come to pass, doubt the fulfilment of that, which so far, seems to be unfulfilled. Do not let us follow in the footsteps of the Jews who claimed to be well versed in the Old Testament, and yet, in spite of the prophecies, persisted in the rejection of Christ.

CHAPTER IV

SOME OF THE PREDICTIONS FOR ISRAEL TO FULFIL

To possess land—the area of which we are told of.

To become a great people—great multiplicity.

To possess a King forever.

To be an everlasting Nation.

To become Sons of the Living God (i.e., Christians).

To dwell in their land for ever.

To have a place appointed for them as their own.

To dwell alone.

The Bible is replete with passages denoting that, however much Almighty God may be displeased with sinful Israel; however much it may be necessary to punish Israel—yet God will extend His mercy, and will "save" Israel in the end.

Opponents to the idea of Israel—as apart from the Jews—*still existing,* are anxious to quote *isolated* texts on which to support their views, and to endeavour to satisfy their own conscience that God *finally* "cast off" Israel; that their deportation to Assyria wiped them off the earth as a nation for ever. That there was an end of them. They quote: "I will no more have mercy upon the House of Israel, but I will utterly take them away." "Then God said, call his name Lo Ammi, for ye are not My people, and I will not be your God" (*Hosea* 1:6-9).

Let these "doubters" read the context, and they will find that God immediately afterwards promises great multiplicity to this self-same Israel: "Where it was said unto them, ye are not My people, there it shall be said unto them ye are the sons of the living God"! A reversal of the utter casting out! There is no confusion, except by taking isolated texts and trying to build up a theory thereon.

If we refer to the 89th Psalm we find it is repeated that God has made a covenant which shall not be broken. Then see II *Chronicles* 7:18: "As I have covenanted with David." God swore an oath *to keep* His covenant: "I have sworn unto David My Servant." How, in the face of this, can we impeach the veracity of God by declaring that Israel was finally "cast off?" Was not the Throne of David to be everlasting? Certainly the Jews have had no King since Zedekiah; therefore the passage cannot refer to the Jews.

When in 587 BC the downfall of Jerusalem came, the temporal kingdom of Judah was destroyed, but *not so* "the seed Royal"; *that* was destined to be preserved, in order that the prophecies might be fulfilled. The promised line from David was to be maintained through the female line—King Zedekiah's daughter.

It is the failure to grasp this significant "sign" that is responsible for much of the unbelief in the Prophetical Books.

Reference to II *Chronicles* 6:16; 7:18; *Jeremiah* 33:17, proves that Israel's kings were to be Judah's tribe *without cessation*, until the coming of the reigning Messiah.

Let us consider what is prophesied in regard to the "future" of Israel, i.e., the "House of Ephraim-Israel"—in the "latter days,"—always bearing in mind that the "birthright," which Esau sold for a mess of pottage, devolved upon *Joseph* (I *Chronicles* 5:1), and not upon any of the other sons of Jacob. Thus, from Joseph the "birthright blessings" descended upon Ephraim; such as—

1. A great and mighty nation (*Genesis* 12:2, and 18:18).

2. Possessing the gate of his enemies (*Genesis* 22:17; 24:60).

3. A nation and a company of nations (*Genesis* 35:11; 48).

4. Under the new covenant and therefore Christians (*Hosea* 1:10; 2:23; *Isaiah* 42:4; 6-8; 16-19; 44:21-22; *Jeremiah* 31:31-34; *Hebrews* 8:8; *Ezekiel* 11:16; 20:35-37; *Zechariah* 10:9).

5. The chief of the nations, Ephraim-Israel (*Jeremiah* 31:7).

6. Manasseh-Israel to be "a great people," but Ephraim-Israel is

to be "greater than he," and is to become "a fulness of nations" (*Genesis* 48:19; *Romans* 11:25).

7. Both of these immensely populous, as "the stars of Heaven" for multitude, as "the sand upon the seashore," as "dust of the earth," and "increasing as fishes do increase" (*Genesis* 22:17; 26:4; 13:16; 48:16; *Isaiah* 10:22; 54:1-3; *Hosea* 1:10).

8. The people of the house of Israel were to be planted in a place of their own, move no more, and to be no more afflicted by "the children of wickedness," their enemies (II *Samuel* 7:10), and there to dwell alone; having been wanderers among the nations (*Hosea* 9:17), from whence they have been sifted out (*Amos* 9:9), and gathered out from among the nations (*Ezekiel* 20:35, 41; *Hosea* 2:14; *Jeremiah* 31:2).

9. In "the islands of the sea" (*Isaiah* 11:11; 24:15); "The isles afar off" (*Jeremiah* 31:10; *Isaiah* 66:19); in the "North country" (*Jeremiah* 3:18; 31:7-8); also in the "West" (*Hosea* 11:10), which is the "appointed place." This place is to become too limited in area for their immensely increasing numbers. "The place is too strait for me" (*Isaiah* 49:20).

10. Pushing the people together to the ends of the earth (*Deuteronomy* 33:17).

11. A great maritime people, whose "seed shall be in many waters," and the chief navigators of the world (*Numbers* 24:7; *Psalm* 89:25).

12. Ephraim-Israel was to be unconquerable as a military power, their national emblems being the Lion and the Unicorn (*Micah* 5:8; Numbers 23:24; 24:9; *Deuteronomy* 33:17; *Genesis* 49:9).

13. A means of blessing to all other nations (*Micah* 5:7; *Genesis* 12:3). Blossoming and budding and filling the face of the world with fruit (*Isaiah* 27:6; 43:7-21; *Matthew* 21:43).

14. God's witnesses to the world and His messenger of salvation to the heathen (*Isaiah* 43:1, 10, 12, 21; 44:1-8).

15. Possessing a great heathen or non-Christian Empire (*Psalm*

111:6).

16. Possessed of enormous wealth, and thereby enabled to lend to all nations, but to borrow of none; and is also to rule over many nations, but never to be ruled over by them (*Deuteronomy* 8:18; 15:6).

17. To possess "the ships of Tarshish," in order to be able to take back their brethren of Judah to Palestine (*Isaiah* 60:9).

18. Observing the Sabbath, thus showing that they possess the "sign of the Sabbath," given only to Israel, as a sign between the Lord and the children of Israel for ever, for a perpetual covenant (*Exodus* 31:13, 16-17; *Ezekiel* 20:12-20).

19. So highly blessed above all people that they are to be known "as the seed whom the Lord hath blessed" (*Isaiah* 61:9).

Let us look round the world to ascertain what nation fulfils all these characteristics—without doubt the choice can *only* fall upon the British Empire. And the world's recent history clearly demonstrates that Israel and the English-speaking races are identical! Great Britain is the "chief of nations" and, with her dominions, constitutes "a company of nations"; "a great people"; "multitudinous"; "planted in the Isles of the West"; "dwelling alone"; "a great maritime people"; "ruling over many and ruled over by none"; etc., etc.

Does not Isaiah address Israel in "the Islands of the Sea" (11:2; 24:15)? "Listen O Isles unto Me, and hearken ye people from afar" (49:1). "The Isles shall wait for Me" (51:5). Great Britain is surely referred to as "the isles afar off."

Great Britain may truly be said to "possess the gate of his enemies"—Great Britain has control of the sea, as the late war has amply proved to the world; Great Britain, as will be shown, possesses a throne descended from David; holds the Sceptre of Judah; and keeps, in Westminster Abbey, Jacob's Stone of Destiny.

That Stone which now reposes under the Coronation Chair in the

Temple of the Lord, at Westminster. On this, in exact accordance with the customs described in the Chronicles of the Kings of Judah, have Kings and Queens been continually crowned. The banner that floats over the keep of Windsor Castle is the Lion of the Tribe of Judah. The Speakers Commentary says: "The Standard of Judah was a lion" (see *Numbers* 23:24, 24:8-9). (Extracted from *British Israel Truth*).

Why, one naturally asks, have the British people in their charge, in Westminster Abbey, this Stone of Destiny? Why did it ever come into the possession of our leading Church? Why was it used for Coronation purposes?

If its history rests only upon outside legends then its use becomes strange, especially with a Nation which prides itself upon being logical in its plans, and fairly level headed.

The Stone is a powerful "sign" to us Britishers of our ancient origin. The possession of, and the use of that Stone goes far to prove the identity of Ephraim-Israel. It has no immediate connection with "the Jews."

We are told in the Bible that Israel is "to inherit the heathen," and also the "uttermost parts of the earth"; and is to be ruled over by "a King of the line of David"—and to be "a Nation forever."Also Israel is destined by God to carry out Christ's Missionary Work among the heathen, a vast responsibility and heritage which can only be carried out by a great and powerful people, and which *is* being exactly fulfilled by the English-speaking races, who possess an evangelising Church for that very purpose; and together they distribute Bibles in all languages by the tens of thousands annually.

CHAPTER V

PROMISES OF LAND

We have the repeated promises of Israel possessing vast portions of the earth's surface in "the last days." "And the Lord appeared unto Abram, and said, Unto thy seed will I give this land" (*Genesis* 12:7).

"In the same day the Lord made a Covenant with Abram, saying, unto thy seed have I given this land from the river of Egypt unto the great river, the river Euphrates." Here we have the boundaries specified in a clear manner!

Purely temporal Blessings of LAND—promised as a BIRTH-RIGHT solely to EPHRAIM-ISRAEL—not to Judah—not to any other sons of Jacob. No, because the Birthright descended to Joseph—and thence to *his* sons solely.

All the promises were repeated on seven separate occasions to Abraham, and again twice to Isaac; and to Jacob. "By Myself have I sworn" (read *Genesis* 22:16-19).

And if one reads carefully *Genesis* 12:1, and *Hebrews* 11:8, we see "By Faith" Abraham obeyed the Lord's Command, not himself knowing whither he went. *Genesis* gives us, fully, details of the areas of LAND falling to Abraham and his seed. All purely temporal and material Promises which cannot be changed, at the will of man, into a "Spiritual Promise"! Nothing can do away with, or set aside the unconditional Promises. St Paul shows this to be impossible. The New Covenant cannot disannul (*Galatians* 3:17), for the New Covenant is of "Grace by Jesus Christ" (*John* 1:17). While St Paul says (*Romans* 15:8), "Jesus Christ was a Minister of the Circumcision for the truth of God to *confirm the promises made to the fathers*."

Therefore the "promises" stand for all time: and consequently Israel must come into actual possession of their heritage on this earth.

Did not St Paul say that "in the last days there shall be those having a form of Godliness *but denying the power thereof ...* ever learning, and never able to come to the knowledge of the truth." This is wonderfully fulfilled in the present age, where we find so many ready to overthrow the prophecies which were "given by inspiration of God," and too ready to doubt the ability of Almighty God to fulfil His promises in any *literal* manner. When we survey the world's history of the past few years, all doubt as to the truth of the "fulfilment" of prophecy is solved: by the simple comparison of prophecy with history.

Dr. Llewellyn Thomas, in *God and My Birthright*, very ably demonstrates as there are *two* Hebrew words for river (one *Nachal* and the other *Nahar*), the former representing a winter torrent such as the El Arish, the latter *Nahar* representing a perpetual river, and which is the actual Hebrew word used in connection with the latter passage, given in *Genesis* 15:18. Thus we know the boundaries lie between the Nile and the Euphrates. All of which has fallen into the hands of, or under the rule of, Great Britain. Why, unless Great Britain be Israel?

Then there is the promise of Israel being a *perpetual* nation. In *Jeremiah* 31:35-36, we are told "If these ordinances (the sun, moon and stars) depart from before Me, saith the Lord, *then* the seed of Israel also *shall cease* from being a *nation* before Me forever."

So, according to God's word, an Israelitish nation *must* exist, and be now existing; and *must* be such a strong nation as will, and does, exactly fulfil the characteristics foretold Israel to possess in the "latter days." It will be found on reference to *Genesis* 49:1 that Jacob is relating that which shall come to pass in "*the last days.*"

Then we have the promise of a *perpetual* line of Kings for Israel—a line unbroken from David until the millennium. This does not fit the Jews.

That Israel shall abandon heathen ways, and following after idols, and seek God, and become "Sons of the living God," i.e.,

Christians. This does not fit the Jews.

We are told that Israel, whose former home was in the Northern provinces of Palestine, was to have "a place appointed"—a "place of their own"—as a safe and permanent home. Read II *Samuel* 7:10: "Moreover I will appoint a place for My people Israel, and will plant them that they may dwell in a place of their own, and move no more, neither shall the children of wickedness afflict them any more as before-time."

Is not this an assurance of Israel existing forever? When this promise was given, Israel inhabited the land allotted to their forefathers, so the place cannot be any of the area of the Promised Land. *That* is to fall to Israel in the "last days." The appointed place must, therefore, be *elsewhere.* God "will plant them." This prophecy does not fit the Jews. They are still wanderers amongst the various nations. Therefore, it can only refer to a living literal "Israel." In the Book of *Isaiah* we are told that Israel is finally to be gathered from "the islands of the sea," hence Israel inhabits islands. We have many references to the "isles of the sea." According to the interpretation of Dr. Llewellyn Thomas, whose book *God and My Birthright* should be read by all persons interested in British-Israel, the words sea and west "are generally the translation of the *same word* in the *Hebrew Bible.*" Therefore, being North and West of Palestine, we can assume that the "islands" are westward of the Mediterranean; the nearest being the British Isles. Refer to *Isaiah* 49:12: "Behold those shall come from far, and lo, these from the north and from the west ...." The British Isles correspond to such a locality, being north and west of Palestine, and from which islands Israel is to be gathered for the re-union of the two Houses of Israel and Judah in the future.

See *Isaiah* 11:11, as to the recovery of "His People" "*from the islands of the sea*"—and remember that the words 'Sea' and 'West' are synonymous (*Kitto's Cyclopedia*).

CHAPTER VI

ISRAEL TO DWELL ALONE

"Lo the people shall dwell alone and shall not be reckoned among the nations" (*Numbers* 23:9). This passage does not refer to the Jews—although they live alone, but scattered over the world—because the Jews ceased to be "a nation" when they crucified Christ.

Israel ceased to be *reckoned* among the nations from the time the Ten Tribes were exiled to captivity. And is not again, *as* "Israel," reckoned among the nations, because Israel is *hidden* from the world as fore-ordained. But we must remember, "Israel," on the other hand, is destined to be a nation "as long as sun, moon and stars exist" (*Jeremiah* 31:36), to be "a great and mighty nation" (*Genesis* 18:18); "High above all nations" (*Deuteronomy* 26:19). These passages guide us to the fact that as the ages pass, Israel is to become more mighty; so great, that in her grandeur she takes a place *alone*; and so above other nations as not to be reckoned with them. Israel, who has been transferred by God to "the appointed place" of safety—the British Isles,—is there any nation that can be compared with England? Certainly, England does not reckon herself in comparison with France, Germany, or Russia, or any other dynasty. England "dwells alone" in that respect. We must remember that the words of the text are taken from Balaam's prophecies, and they relate to a people in a condition of blessedness, and not to a people suffering still from the curse—as are the Jews. It refers to the Ten-Tribed House of Israel, and of them it can truly be said "the Lord, his God, is with him, and the shout of a king is among them." The Jews have no king. Then again, "He hath, as it were, the strength of an unicorn: Behold the people shall rise up as a great lion, and lift himself up as a young lion." All this is applicable to Israel, but not so to Judah—a people in dispersion. Much of the confusion in the minds of people is solely because they fail to see the distinction between Israel and Judah. Until they grasp this difference, they cannot intelligibly interpret the prophetical books of the Old Testament. Never lose sight of the fact that by God's word Israel has to be a nation *forever*. Is never "to cease from being a nation before Me forever." This is definite and clear. No one has any scriptural authority to alter this plain statement, or to say it means a "spiritual Israel"; or that it means "the Church," for they cannot support such a view. Does not Balaam tell us that "Israel is to eat up the nations—his enemies"? This expression can only refer to a great and conquering nation, not to the few million of Jews on the earth.

"And who is like Thy people Israel, a nation that *is alone* in the earth whom God went to redeem?"

"He hath not dealt so with any nation" (*Psalm* 147:20). There is no other nation to compare with Israel which is represented by "the Stone Kingdom," which is destined to overcome all other nations, and fill the whole earth. The British Isles representing the "stone cut out" (of the mountain of Europe) without hands.

CHAPTER VII

THE STONE KINGDOM

In *Daniel* 2 we are given Daniel's interpretation of Nebuchadnezzar's Dream Image; the King was surprised by the appearance in his dream of a stone, cut out without hands, which smote the image upon his feet that were of iron and clay, and brake them to pieces.

The interpretation is, that Nebuchadnezzar himself represents the head of gold of this image. God had given him a kingdom with power, strength, and glory.

After Nebuchadnezzar was to arise another kingdom, inferior; followed by a third, and a fourth.

Then comes the interpretation: And in the days of these four earthly monarchs, "The God of Heaven shall set up a kingdom, which shall never be destroyed; and the kingdom shall not be left to other people, but it shall break in pieces and consume all these kingdoms, and it shall stand for ever."

From this we can clearly see that God Himself set up a fifth, and *final* kingdom. It was to have no successor, it is to stand for ever.

The first of the four monarchies was Babylon, under King Nebuchadnezzar; the next was Medo-Persia, followed by Greece and then Rome. All these were, in turn, to be destroyed. The mission of the fifth was to destroy them (the image) and to fill the world.

This mission exactly corresponds with that of Israel, which was to be a nation *forever*. So we may take it for granted that Israel, the Stone Kingdom, and Great Britain, *are identical*. The kingdom holding the *perpetual* Throne of David until He comes whose right it is.

Nebuchadnezzar saw *no hands* cutting out the stone, out of the mountain, which is symbolical with Israel's unidentified journey through the world during the past centuries. Israel has, through Divine plan, gone forward from Assyrian exile, to the "place appointed," as the nation *set up by God Himself* to overthrow all other nations, and eventually to fill the whole earth. To fulfil the prophecy that "Abraham is heir to the world." Through such marvellous Divine plan Israel, under the name of Britain, has been able to rise to her greatness, and to "dwell alone," in the safety of the British Isles, unrecognised by her neighbouring nations, and consequently unenvied by them during her progress.

All this concealment has been aided through the eyes of commentators, theologians, and teachers being "blinded," and as they in olden days (the early days of Christianity) could—naturally—see no nation on the earth likely to rival in power the great Roman Empire, they were unable to account for the dream in any other manner than that the Stone Kingdom and Israel (lost to them) were intended to be but symbolical of "the Church." What else, thought they, could it be? The more one looks at this, the more improbable it becomes! It was excusable in the fourth or fifth centuries (AD). But now, when one sees the old prophecies being fulfilled to Britain as were "promised" to Israel, there is no excuse for cultivating "out of date" theories such as these.

It *cannot* refer to "the Church," because the actual words of Holy Scripture say: "*In the days of these kings*" the kingdom shall be set up. Christianity was not "set up" until the days of the last of the four earthly kingdoms, i.e., in the days of the Roman Empire. What had "the Church" to do with the destruction of Babylon, or Medo-Persia, or Greece? Did the Church either take any part in the fall of the Roman Empire? The whole argument is fallacious. Then again, there is no solidarity with "the Church"; it is broken up into many religious bodies holding diverse views—no uniformity. In these circumstances, we are compelled to realise that the words of Holy Scripture are surely here intended to be taken in their literal sense. The fifth, or Stone Kingdom, is as much an earthly or material kingdom, as the four which preceded it; Israel was existing when Babylon arose, and also during the existence of each of the four monarchies in succession; and Israel fulfils to the very letter the words of the prophecy. Israel, the Stone Kingdom, and Great Britain are identical. How otherwise is Britain now in occupation of Palestine, and of most—if not all— of the Promised Land? Is Britain a "Gentile nation," still treading down Jerusalem? If so, it stands to reason Israel has yet to be discovered to turn the British out of Palestine, Egypt, Africa, India, the Oversea Dominions, and all other possessions, and to break our sea power in the world! This is certain, because Israel in the "last days" is prophesied to be the holder of all these birthright blessings promised to the descendants of Joseph. Since Britain has (often unwillingly it is true) come into possession of all the promises, we may be certain Britain is Israel under the predicted change of name and language.

Bear in mind that if Britain is *not* Israel, Britain must be destroyed, for *only* Israel is to be exempted,—"though I make a full end of the Nations whither I have driven thee (Israel) yet will I not make a full end of thee" (*Jeremiah* 30:11). Britain, if not Israel must be one of the "all nations" who are to be gathered against Jerusalem, and who are to be "broken in pieces" *by Israel* (*Joel* 3:2, 12, 14; *Zechariah* 12:9; *Jeremiah* 51:20).

THE KINGDOM

The dream of King Nebuchadnezzar, King of Babylon, was in the second year of his reign (*Daniel* 2:1), "Thou art this head of gold" (verse 38). That is, Nebuchadnezzar was the ruler of the first of four monarchies. The date would be 604 BC. If "seven times" punishment was to run, equal to 2,520 solar years, it would mean 2,520—604=1917 AD as being the termination of that "seven times." By this time it would have run its course, and in the very year in which Jerusalem and Palestine were released, by the British, from Turkish control.

We are told by the prophet Zechariah (chaps. 12, 14) that Israel and Judah shall *both* be in occupation of Palestine when Christ comes.

If the British be not Israel, is it but a mere coincidence that Britain has been given a mandate over Palestine, and is repatriating the Jews? They are now both in Palestine! Is it a coincidence that Britain has dislodged the Gentile Turks—or Edom—when Israel was to do it?

When we remember that before this could happen Israel was *to change name and language* the fact surely becomes more than "a coincidence"!

CHAPTER VIII

THE NEW COVENANT

In regard to the making of the New Covenant, see *Jeremiah* 31:31:

"Behold the days come saith the Lord, that I will make a new covenant with the House of Israel and with the House of Judah."

Many opponents at once say: "How could a new covenant be made if the two houses were apart?" God said He would "make" it, and St Paul says that the Mosaic covenant had been "made" old; thereby, Christ made the New Covenant through the sacrifice of Himself, and to participate in the fruits of that sacrifice (of Himself) it was no more necessary for Israel to be on the spot than for the Chinese to be there.

Even Judah was only represented in Palestine *then* by a fragment of the people, and there was also (loaned to the Jews) a fragment of Israel present, viz., the tribe of Benjamin, which belonged to the House of Joseph (II *Samuel* 19:20), that is, to the "House of Israel," but was "attached" to Judah at the time. (See *Lost and Found* by J. G. Taylor).

The Jews as yet have not accepted Christ; that they will, ultimately, is certain, after the re-union, and then Holy Scriptures will be fulfilled as regards the *two* houses. How could the new covenant be made with the two houses if the House of Israel (of the Ten Tribes) *ceased to exist,* as the House of Judah was not then ready for it?

Thus, as Mr. Taylor points out, "to find Israel a Christian nation, i.e., under the new covenant, is to vindicate *Hebrews* 8:10; while the unbelief and deposition of the Jews is a vindication of *Matthew* 21:43.

It may be well to refer here to the confusion which exists as to the word "Gentiles." It surely refers to those people outside the covenant made with Abraham, Isaac and Jacob. The uncovenanted people. To the Jews, in our Lord's day, all who were not Jews were classed Gentiles, and similarly to the Romans all outside of their Empire were Gentiles.

But this fact does not make the Northern Kingdom of Israel a "Gentile nation."

CHAPTER IX

WHY "SPIRITUALISE" ISRAEL?

Then we have that large body of opponents who will "spiritualise" Israel. The advice given by the Rev. G. H. Lancaster is: "If you spiritualise Israel, you must be fair and spiritualise the Jews also; to say nothing of other empires who were contemporary with Israel, such as Babylon." *Matthew* 21:43 shows that it is no more possible to "spiritualise" the "nation" to whom the Kingdom of God was given than to spiritualise the Jews from whom it was taken. (N.B.—Christ said "nation," *not* "Church.") There is no justification for changing the word *nation* to "Church." The word in the original Greek is "*nation*." British-Israel truth is a wonderful *proof* of the inspiration of the Bible, and to the greatest evidence of Christianity.

Therefore British-Israelites, as they can find no word in Holy Scripture to justify any "spiritualising," cannot possibly accept such teaching. The error has apparently been perpetuated from the days of the third or fourth century AD, and has, unfortunately, become accepted as "a matter of course," therefore it behoves all of us who desire to read the Bible aright, to *unlearn* much of our early day teaching—or in the words of Antisthenes: "The most needful piece of learning for the uses of Life is to unlearn what is untrue." Dr. Isaac Watts said: "The greatest part of the Christian world can hardly give any reason *why* they believe the Bible to be the Word of God, *but because they have always believed it, as they were taught so from their infancy.*"

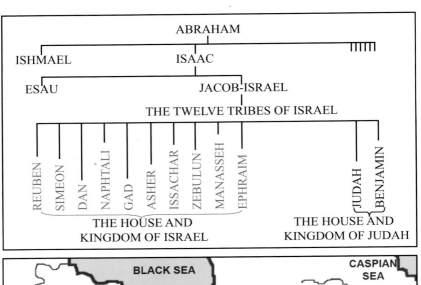

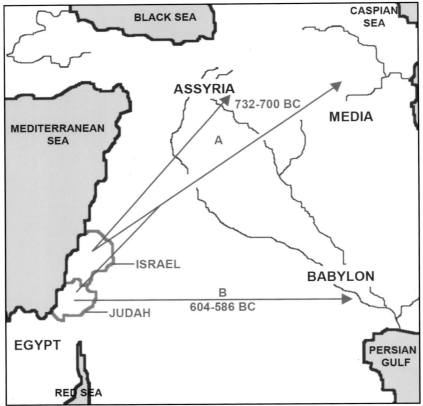

Mount Zion in the Caucasus mountain range

Travelling north towards the Caucasus following the river.
Note the wide flat bed of the river that could easily handle the migrations
of Israel with all their livestock

CHAPTER X

ISRAEL'S WANDERINGS

The wanderings of Israel after their escape from Assyria can be traced historically from the region of Euphrates to Britain, covering a period of over one thousand years; and the prophetical writings of the Old Testament are the history of the British race from the days when Shem lived. For remember, little or nothing is recorded of the descendants of Noah's other two sons Ham and Japhet.

Esdras has recorded the migration of the Israelites to Arsareth, and several other ancient writers confirm this. The banishment of the House of Israel was for a Divine purpose, for we read in I *Chronicles* 5:26 that "the God of Israel stirred up the spirit of Pul, King of Assyria." But the Bible gives evidence that this removal did not mean *extinction.* They were to be a nation "for ever." God had appointed a place for them, where they should dwell and move no more (read II *Samuel* 7:10). God also said: "I will multiply thy seed as the stars of the heavens, and as the sand which is upon the sea-shore." This proves Israel was TO LIVE, not to become extinct.

If we follow the history we can trace the wanderings of the Ten Tribes from Media to Britain in three separate divisions, and becoming recognised as the Getae and the Massagetae, the Azar, and the Angles—known also as the Ostrogoths and the Normans. Anyone who desires an interesting history of the wanderings should procure a copy of *The Origin of the English* by Major B. de W. Weldon MC, the author also of that valuable work *The Evolution of Israel.*

God's partial rejection, for a time, of Israel was, in effect, a decree of Gentilization, brought about by the tribes being thrown among heathen races and broken up—condemned to be "Wanderers" (*Hosea* 9:17).

CHAPTER XI

GOD'S PROMISES TO ISRAEL

Let us, in considering the question of Israel, always bear in mind that in God's promises to Abraham we have a trinity of blessings:

1. His seed should become a great nation, and they should inherit the land of Canaan (*Genesis* 13:15).

2. He should be the progenitor of the coming of Christ (*Galatians* 3:16).

3. He should be the father of many nations, of multitudes of peoples; they should possess the ends of the earth, and the gate of their enemies (*Genesis* 22:17).

All was, in these promises, transmitted to Isaac and to Jacob, and to Jacob's twelve sons.

The first and second promises were literally made good to the most minute details of His life, death and resurrection.

The third promise must be as truly and literally fulfilled as the first and second.

And now let us ask ourselves upon whose authority are we to take two literally, but to spiritualise the third? Is there one word in Holy Scripture to justify such a course? Why, if we know two were literally fulfilled, should we not logically and reasonably expect the third promise to be also literal.

If the curses are literal, surely the blessings will be equally literal? If the past be literal, why not the future predictions? If you spiritualise Israel, why not do the same with Judah?

Do let us remember that upon Joseph's sons descended the birthright (*Hebrews* 11:21) thus, if this fact be borne in mind, we shall hear less of Palestine belonging to "the Jews."

1. Jacob first declared that the possessor of the birthright should grow into a multitude in the midst of the earth.

2. That "the branches should run over the wall"; which is, of

truth, applicable first to the United States of America, who broke away and spread abroad; and then, as many of the British have also done, "to people" our great Dominions overseas. They had to expand for lack of room for their great population.

3. That his hands would be made strong, and that he would shepherd the Stone of Israel.

4. That God would bless him with the blessings of Heaven above, the blessings of the deep.

5. The blessings of the breast and womb, so that the multitude might be born and reared as strong, healthy individuals.

All these blessings were bequeathed to Joseph's two sons, and thence to the British race, who, from all the signs which are given to us, can be none other than the Children of Israel *under another name*.

Joseph, when he was in Egypt, was not recognisable by his brethren; so it is equally possible for "Israel" of to-day to be unidentified, or hidden, but not "lost" to the extent of being extinct.

There is a little coincidence—which many will look upon as a mere coincidence—in the fact, that at the top of the page in the Book of *Genesis*, where God definitely promises land to the seed of Abraham, the date is there given as being BC 1918. Great Britain took Palestine, the very centre of the Promised Land, from the Gentiles (the Turks), 1917. And from which latter date Jerusalem has "ceased to be trodden down of the Gentiles." This is given as an interesting fact in the study of the prophecies being fulfilled.

CHAPTER XII

ISRAEL AND "BLINDNESS" OF IDENTITY

Our nation, by the decree of God, is made "blind" to their origin. St Paul sets before the Gentile Christians "that blindness in part is happened to Israel until the fulness of the Gentiles be come in." This part of Israel, before mentioned as broken off, is *blind*, and will remain so until Ephraim's promised fulness, referred to in *Genesis* 48:19, be accomplished.

Do we not read in *Isaiah* 29:11-12: "Read this, I pray thee, and he saith, I cannot, for it is sealed?" Then again, in *Daniel* 12:8-9: "Go thy way, Daniel, for the words are closed up and sealed."

There is a reason, of course, for all this concealment, but the time is at hand for the eyes to be opened. Read *Isaiah* 42:18-19: "Hear, ye deaf; and look, ye blind, that ye may see. Who is blind, but My servant? or deaf as My Messenger that I sent? Who is blind as he that is perfect; and blind as the Lord's servant? Seeing many things, but thou observest not; opening the ears, but he heareth not." Then turn to *Romans* 11:25: "... that blindness in part is happened to Israel until the fulness of the Gentiles be come in." And then, in the following verse comes the message of hope: "And so all Israel shall be saved, as it is written, There shall come out of Zion the Deliverer, and shall turn away ungodliness from Jacob."

"His watchmen are blind" (*Isaiah* 56:10). "For the Lord hath poured out upon you the Spirit of deep sleep and hath closed your eyes" (*Isaiah* 29:10).

In a desire amongst so many to read St Paul's Epistle to the Romans, especially chapters 9, 10, 11, as relating to "the Jews," Bible students fail to realise that the Jews are mentioned but thrice, while Israel is referred to some fourteen times. Paul by inspiration wrote cautiously, in order not to disclose that which God designed to be concealed until the fulness of time.

CHAPTER XIII

THE APOSTLES' JOURNEYS

It is possible that some of the Apostles found their way to localities north and west of the Black Sea, to Arsareth, whither, according to Esdras and other historians, the Ten Tribes had migrated. They would endeavour to do so in order to preach the Gospel, as commanded "to the dispersed tribes of Israel." "Go not into the way of the Gentiles (i.e., to others than of Israel), and into any city of the Samaritans enter ye not" (*Matthew* 10:5-6). "Then said the Jews among themselves, whither will He go that we shall not find Him?" "Will He go unto the *dispersed* among the Gentiles?" "And teach the Gentiles?" The Samaritans were, by origin, a mixed heathen people, whom the King of Assyria had sent to inhabit Samaria after he had carried the Israelites captive (II *Kings* 17:24-41). Christ's many references to the "lost sheep of the House of Israel," no doubt referred to the hidden exiled Ten Tribes whom God had destined should rise to such immense power in the world. Is it not more than likely, therefore, that the Apostles made their way to the Israelites, who by that time were living and known as the Getae and who, later, were known as the Goths? If you refer to *Isaiah* 9:1-7, it will be found that Israel, a heathen and a Gentile people, are to see a great light in their darkness. The Getae lapsed into heathenism. A deliverer was promised; they—the Israelites, under a changed name—would, we read, be led to "a glorious land."

When we refer to *Acts* 2 it is found that St Peter's distinction between "Jew" and "men of Israel" is as distinct as in the Old Testament. It would be about AD 28 that our Lord despatched His Apostles upon their mission to "the lost sheep of the House of Israel"; and a few years later, about AD 61 we find St Peter writing to the strangers "scattered" in the Black Sea district (I *Peter* 1:1). He addresses them as "elect," i.e., "Chosen of God." Israel now passes

51

from the "Lo ammi" (forsaken) stage and is henceforward called by the name of God once more. "The Chosen" were first Judah, from 530 BC, until AD 33. Thence onwards the Israelites became "The Chosen." "Sheep" is an expression frequently made use of as representative of Israel—as "New Wine" is expressive of "The Gospel."

"The Jews" were not Christ's sheep, for our Lord said: "Ye believe not because ye are not My Sheep." From the Bible we learn that the lost sheep of the House of Israel are the elect who are sojourners of the Dispersion. This seems to be clear from *Isaiah* 9:2; *Hosea* 2:23; *Matthew* 4:13-16; *Luke* 1:79; I *Peter* 2:10. Those who had not obtained mercy but *now* have obtained mercy. The Elect, being Israel, are the very people to whom Christ sent forth His Disciples (see *Matthew* 10:6; 15:24).

Then if we refer to *Zechariah* 10 there can be no doubt, or mistake, for we read: "I will strengthen the House of Judah, and I will *save* the House of Joseph ... and they (of Joseph) shall be as though I had not cast them off."

CHAPTER XIV

REVERSING THE SENTENCE ON ISRAEL

In I *Peter* 2 we find a reversal of the sentence which had centuries before been imposed through the Prophet Hosea, upon Israel. Ephraim, through turning to God, was at last becoming fitted to be "a corner stone," "a chosen generation ... which had not obtained mercy, but now have obtained mercy."

This was written about AD 61, and almost immediately after this we find mention in Pliny and Tacitus, of the Goths. For years the Israelites had been "outcasts," rejected by God, yet it was witnessed of these people that they *were to be* called by the name of God, as it had also been written: "Ye shall *not* be called by My Name." Here God's mercy intervenes. The syllable "Got" in Goth is the name of God; as is the syllable "El" in Israel.

"In the place where it was said unto them, Ye are not My People, there it shall be said unto them, Ye are the Sons of the Living God" (*Hosea* 1:10, 785 BC).

This is a definite promise of God's *forgiveness*. It is His merciful *reversal* of His former sentence that Israel *should cease* from being "His people." It is the saving them from the Lo Ammi Stage. "Hath God cast away His people?" refers to Israel, and not to the Jews. So this answer of "God forbid" is our assurance of the *Everliving* Nation of Israel. It is not, it cannot, in the face of these words, be "cast away" or "lost"! The prophet Zechariah in the words quoted above tells us so "for our learning."

"For a small moment have I forsaken thee; but with great mercies will I gather thee. In a little wrath I hid My face from thee for a moment; but with everlasting kindness will I have mercy on thee, saith the Lord thy Redeemer" (*Isaiah* 54:7-8). This proves there was no final casting off of the Northern Kingdom.

CHAPTER XV

CHANGE OF NAME

About AD 106 the name of Goth is much heard of in Roman history; while Greek and Roman historians regard the Getae and the Goths as the same people.

Dr. Bradley in his *Story of the Nations* relates how the locality north of the Danube mouth was inhabited by a people called the Getae. In the third century AD the Goths came, and the Romans looked upon the Goths and Getae as one people.

The word Goth is derived from Guta Thead a people of God. Dr. Bradley's book tells us these two peoples were similar in appearance. They were a people *in,* but not of Scythia. The Goths were, doubtless, the tribes of Israel (of "Joseph's House"). The words Israel, Goth, Asar, Angle, all contain the root word "God"; all mean the same, and were adopted on the cessation of the "Lo ammi" (or forsaken) period; on the return (as was promised) of Israel, *from God's disfavour.* During that period of disfavour the Israelites abandoned the name of "El" (or "God"); so we see Hosea's prophecy: "I will no more have mercy upon the House of Israel" fulfilled for a period during which time the Israelites were *not* "God's People"; "Ye are not My people," said the Lord, through Hosea, "and I will not be your God" (1:9). This sentence, however, was *not* to be *permanent*; *Ezekiel* 4 implies that the term of Israel's punishment will last for 390 years, from the fall of Samaria until 330 BC, which was two centuries later than the return from Babylon. No renewal of Divine favour could possibly be expected until long after the days of Cyrus. There is no reason to suppose that the intention of Cyrus, who overthrew the Babylonian monarchy (as related by *Ezra* 1:1-3) went beyond the Jews. Cyrus could hardly have in his mind, or have any knowledge of the northern Israelites deported to Assyria. As regards the preordained change of name, as pointed out above, we see the Scriptures fulfilled in the changed name, as we also see it fulfilled in "the scattering," for Israel was to be "scattered among the Nations" and "sifted" through them "like as corn is sifted in a sieve, yet shall not the least grain (margin "Stone") fall upon the earth."

The Rev. J. H. Allen, of America, says: "The reason that 'Stone' is used in the margin is because it is the true rendering, but 'grain' is used in the text so as not to mix the metaphor. National Israel is the Stone Kingdom in the natural—in the flesh—but the Kingdom of Heaven preached by Our Lord, by John the Baptist, and the Apostles, is the Spiritual Stone Kingdom. Jacob's pillow-pillar Stone is the type of the earthly Stone Kingdom, but the Stone which the Jewish Builders rejected is the Spiritual Corner, or foundation Stone of the Spiritual Stone Kingdom of *Daniel* 2:34-44."

CHAPTER XVI

DID ISRAEL RETURN TO PALESTINE?—NO!

The question is, were the Israelites invited to return? Did they return? In *Ezra* 1:5, we have a brief description of the *returning* captives:

1. Judah,
2. Benjamin,
3. the Priests,
4. the Levites,
5. "all those whose spirit God stirred up."

Judah and Benjamin, as "tribes," are not mentioned in verse 1, it is "heads of father's houses of Judah and Benjamin." There is no evidence that these included a single Israelite of the "Northern Kingdom." The next chapter of *Ezra* affords more details (see 2:1), which is convincing proof that those who went back were limited to Jews, Levites, and Benjamites, for it shows they belonged to "*the province*." Their ancestors, who had been removed to Babylon, were Jews *only*. The Ten Tribes had been exiled to Assyria, to Gozan and Media. "They *returned* (or came again R.V.) unto Jerusalem and Judea"; importing that they, or their fathers, *previously* dwelt there, which would not have been true of the Israelites. "They returned everyone unto his city" the Northern Tribes had no cities *in Judah*. Their cities were in the land of Israel (see *Lost and Found* by J. G. Taylor).

Those who returned (says Ezra) were they "Whom Nebuchad-nezzar had carried away to Babylon"—only the House of Judah, with the Benjamites, were taken to Babylon.

Not a word is said about the return of Israel, who, over a century earlier, had been exiled to Assyria and where the Old Testament leaves their history.

We have ample proof of the *non-return* of the tribes of the Northern Kingdom to Palestine with the Jews, besides *Ezra* 2; for the Books of the *Chronicles* were compiled *after* the Jews, with the Benjamites, returned from *their* Babylonish Captivity. In I *Chronicles* 5:26, we are told that the "Northern Kingdom" were *then, at the time of writing, in captivity; so the author knew of no return!* The Book of II *Esdras* states *definitely* that they *did not* return to Palestine, but that they moved to Arsareth. This is good historical proof. The Book of *Nehemiah* records the genealogies of those who returned, but makes no mention of the Ten Tribes from Assyria. The Prophet Zechariah, writing 18 years after the Jews returned from Babylon would certainly not have written as he did (10:6-9) had the twelve tribes been reunited. Had they returned would not the tribes have claimed their ancient possessions (II *Kings* 17:24; *John* 4:9), which were then in possession of others? Therefore what became of these tribes? Zechariah states that God will have mercy upon the House of Joseph, "they shall be as though I had *not* cast them off" (10:6). This is also remarked upon in *Romans* 9:26. The "House of Joseph" *must not* be confused with the "House of Judah," a mistake so many make.

What does the Historian say? Josephus the Jewish Historian is clear and decisive in writing AD 70, for he says: "The Ten Tribes *did not* return to Palestine: only Two Tribes served the Romans after Palestine became a Roman Province." No historical evidence can be more conclusive. So we may be quite satisfied that the Northern Kingdom did *not* return to their former cities with the Jews "as tribes." There is no record of the Northern Kingdom amalgamating with Judah *in captivity*, and the Bible does not support such an idea. Rather the contrary, because the Bible gives quite a separate historical "future" for "Ephraim Israel" to that for "Judah." God's Word gives us plainly, those people who did return to Palestine. This being so, what became of Israel? As God said, *and repeated*, that Israel would be an "Everlasting" Nation,—Israel, we *know*, must exist upon the earth.

The theory which some teach that the Israelites are merged into the Jews is knocked to pieces by *Zechariah* 11:10: "And I took My Staff even Beauty, and cut it asunder, that I might break My Covenant which I had made with all the people."

The Brotherhood between Israel and Judah was broken when Christ was betrayed and crucified. They are separate to this day—on the authority of God's Word.

Dean Farrar writes, that with the exception of Judas Iscariot the twelve Apostles were Benjamites, and therefore *not* "Jews" by race. This view is confirmed in *Acts* 1:11; 2:7, which show them to be Galileans.

The Rev. Merton Smith, having asked the Chief Rabbi (from the "Covenant People"):

1. Are the people known as the Jews throughout the world the descendants of Judah and Levi, or is there a known admixture of other tribes?

2. If so, in what proportion, and what authority is there for saying so?

3. If not, what has become of the other Tribes, and where, according to your knowledge, are they?

4. If that is unknown, where were they when Judah last knew of them? Does the orthodox Judaism still look for the recovery of the twelve tribes at some future date?

The following is the reply:

"Office of the Chief Rabbi,
"November 18th, 1918.

"In reply to your letter of 15th inst. I am desired by the Chief Rabbi to State:

1. The people known at present as Jews are descendants of the tribes of Judah and Benjamin, with a certain number of descendants of the tribe of Levi.
2. As far as is known there is not any further admixture of other tribes.
3. The ten tribes have been absorbed among the Nations of the world (see II *Kings*, chap. 17, more especially verses 22-23).
4. We look forward to the gathering of all the tribes at some future day (see *Isaiah* 27:12-13, and *Ezekiel* 37:15-18)."

Signed by the Chief Rabbi's Secretary.

This is a complete answer to those who still vainly imagine and constantly so preach—that the ten tribes became intermingled with the Jews at the time the latter returned to Palestine from their seventy years of Captivity. This is the pronouncement of one who is at the head of the Kingdom of Judah and cannot lightly be ignored.

CHAPTER XVII

GOD'S MERCY ON ISRAEL IS FORETOLD

Severed from the Old Covenant, they were to be replaced in Divine favour by the new (*Jeremiah* 31:33; *Hebrews* 8:10-13; *Hosea* 2:23; I *Peter* 2:10). Strewn about though they were for a while God *would* afterwards re-unite them, and gather them into "a land of their own" (II *Samuel* 7:10; *Jeremiah* 31:10), so they are settled somewhere under a Gentile guise. (See *Lost and Found* by J. G. Taylor).

Having been scattered, and afterwards gathered "into a place of their own," prophecy is again fulfilled. God shows His mercy (see *Hosea* 1:10): "... it shall come to pass that in the place where it was said unto them ye are not My people, there it shall be said unto them, 'Ye are the sons of the living God,'" i.e., believers in Christ; see also *Hosea* 14:4-6: "I will heal their backsliding, I will love them freely, for My anger is turned away from him... ." (See also *Romans* 9:26).

Then turn to *Jeremiah* 30:3, 10-11; *Jeremiah* 31:36-37; 33:7 (and there are many other references of God showing mercy where He had previously threatened expulsion), but probably, enough has been quoted to make it clear that the Ten Tribes left their worship of idols, and turned to God, accepted Christ, and were restored to favour as God's "Chosen People" in place of the Jews, from whom Christ took the kingdom, and bestowed it upon Israel. And now Israel and Judah can look forward to their coming reunion, and *all* serving as *one* nation, under *one head,* and shall not be two nations any more, as prophecy predicts.

CHAPTER XVIII

THE CHURCH OF ENGLAND

In that most excellent work, *The Evolution of Israel* by Major B. de W. Weldon, MC, we have an ably argued statement that the Church is the "Established Church," and its Prayer Book, officially a Schedule of an Act of Parliament, expressing by law the religious opinion of the nation.

The Anglican Church being the Church of the People of Israel—and the whole ritual reads as such,—the congregations repeat that God's promises and curses to Israel have been fulfilled to *our* nation, and to *our* forefathers. Look at the many references; in the "Benedictus" for example, we repeat: "Blessed be the Lord God of Israel, who hath visited and *redeemed* His People." The Jews are not yet redeemed! They have rejected the Trinity in Unity. Then, in the Athanasian Creed we repeat: "And the Catholic Faith is this, that we worship one God in Trinity, and Trinity in Unity."

If we examine the Venite, Te Deum, Magnificat, Cantate, we find them replete with Israelitish references. It is only to be understood if the worshipping congregations are the descendants of Ephraim-Israel! The references cannot be any coincidence; they must be given as "a sign" for guidance, of our undoubted connection with Israel. If *not,* the whole service is meaningless! All this was arranged in the days of the Reformation. It is the people who attend the Church services who are "blind" as to their origin. Open their eyes, and the meaning of our form of service is intelligible to them.

It will become clear to the minds of all those who study this question—and it is well worthy of study by even the greatest opponents—that the words used in our Church Services have designedly a great lesson for us regarding our Nation's ancestry and of our direct descent from Israel. Take the versicles following the Creed: "O Lord save Thy people, and bless Thine inheritance. And make Thy Chosen people joyful." If they do not refer to a race descended from Israel, "God's Chosen People," why do we nationally so address Almighty God in our Church Service?

When one carefully considers such passages as *Hosea* 2:23; I *Peter* 2:10; *Isaiah* 9:2; *Luke* 1:70; *Matthew* 4:13-16, it seems to be clearly evident that Israel are the "Elect" referred to. Those "which, in times past were not a people, but are *now* the people of God, which had not obtained mercy, but *now* have obtained mercy."

Those people to whom Jesus Christ referred to as "the lost sheep of the House of Israel" (*Matthew* 10:6), the people to whom, in their wanderings, Our Lord sent His Disciples. The people destined to preach the gospel throughout the ages in all lands to try and gather souls to Christ.

Then what a lesson the "Benedictus" teaches us—Jesus coming to His "heritage," His "Sheep," His "Witnesses" His "people Israel" (nothing here of the "Jews") speaking through the prophets to a *future* "Israel," promising them "Safety" and fulfilment of all God's promises to the Fathers.

Why should the English people pray for deliverance from their enemies when the promise was only given to Israel?

Why is it that the laws of Britain and the United States are framed upon the Hebrew laws of Moses? Surely it can only be explained because we are the descendants of the Nation Israel.

We cannot argue away such potent facts: much as we, nationally, are in the main quite willing to transfer Israel to being now "the Church."

No—rather is it, that "the Church" is but the means employed by the Nation Israel for evangelising the heathen—and converting the Jews. Why do we use Hebrew weights and measures? Why use so many Hebrew roots in our language? There is but one answer. Because Israel and the English-speaking races are identical.

CHAPTER XIX

THE TEACHINGS OF THE COMMENTATORS

Is the teaching of our clergy and theologians sound? If we refer to *Revelation* 17 we find the word "mystery" referred to; mystery means, in the Greek, "to shut the eyes," and so the Church, by their teaching, have shut the eyes of the people. Babylon means "confusion." How great is the "confusion" in the Christian religion. It is time for Israel to awake, for the "seven times" of the Gentile rule is expiring: Jerusalem has already been redeemed from the Turk; and Judah is going back to her own land to become, once more, a nation under the protectorate of Great Britain (Israel). Judah and Israel (the two sticks of *Ezekiel* 37) are to be rejoined, to become one nation with one king. The Apostle to the Romans warned all that "blindness *in part* had happened to Israel, *until* the fulness of the Gentiles be come in." Now the blindness is falling off Israel, and the "lost sheep" (the Ten Tribes) are being found. At this time there is a "shaking" among the "dry bones," trying to find God and His plans. There are many "signs" given to us, whereby we may *find* the Ten Tribes. Chiefly in England and America—Joseph's seed—and they are "the ten thousands of Ephraim and the thousands of Manasseh."

The ancient commentators when they first laid the basis of what is our present-day teaching could see no living nation comparable with the greatness foreshadowed for a Nation Israel. Here is the point where our early teaching went astray. To try and make God's promises to Israel intelligible "the Church" was looked upon as having replaced the literal Israel thought to be extinct.

The time has come for the world to awaken from such a fancy. The curriculum of our Universities and Theological Colleges needs revision so as to get out of a wrong groove of thought and teaching, for what was excusable in the fourth century AD is inexcusable now.

The masses need a lead, but it will be a matter of—"For precept upon precept, precept upon precept, line upon line, line upon line, here a little and there a little ..." To keep on impressing the need of a change of interpretation in the reading of the prophecies, before the eyes of the blind will be opened. There is "a time for everything" and the time for this change of thought is rapidly approaching.

CHAPTER XX

KEEPING THE SABBATH

One of the "signs" for our guidance is the fact that the keeping of the Sabbath was to be a *sign* between the Lord and Israel: "Wherefore the children of Israel shall keep the Sabbath to observe the Sabbath throughout their generations, for a perpetual Covenant. It is a sign between Me and the Children of Israel for ever" (*Exodus* 31:16-17). See also *Ezekiel* 20:20.

Only the British race acknowledge the Sabbath by law. Is it not the special privilege of the Anglo-Saxon race—*alone among the Nations*—to observe Sunday as God's Day? They, unless wilfully blind, can surely see that such "a sign" was a special gift *to* our race for a purpose. Therefore, why go out of one's way, as some do, to argue that so long as one attends an early Communion it is immaterial how the rest of the Sabbath day be kept. Or, again, why depart from the custom of the past by only reading the Commandments to the Communicants, or those who may attend that Special Service?

Such acts contribute towards carelessness in the keeping of the Sabbath.

Israel is to be "heir of the world," and is to subdue all other nations, and to keep in perpetuity the Throne of David until Christ comes to reign on earth during the millennium.

Thus we have Israel to endure *for ever*, and we have the "Stone Kingdom" to destroy all other nations, and "to break in pieces and consume all those kingdoms." "*And it shall be for ever!*" To perform the same thing. BOTH to be everlasting! Thus both identical with Great Britain.

"Truly we see not our signs" (*Psalm* 74:9). "Ye shall keep My Sabbaths" (*Leviticus* 26:2).

CHAPTER XXI

"THE THRONE OF DAVID"

ISRAEL THE STRONG NATION WITH DAVID'S THRONE

The continuity of the direct line of David's throne has never been broken, it *never can* be broken, for it is "everlasting." Holy Scripture is clear and emphatic upon this, and "The Scriptures cannot be broken" (*John* 10:35).

We know from *Micah* 4:7, Israel was never to be ultimately *lost*, for do we not read: "I will make her that was cast off a strong nation?" When this message was delivered by Micah, Israel was in *captivity,* whereas the Jews were in Palestine. Therefore, while Judah was destined to become "a remnant," "cast off" Israel was to become a "strong nation." This promise is definite, and so must be fulfilled. Then, if more proof be needed, are we not told: "I will bring again the captivity of My people Israel ... I will plant them upon their land" (*Amos* 9:14-15).

The Prophet Jeremiah, in chapter 31:18-20, teaches us that Ephraim-Israel *would repent* of their evil ways, and would be re-instated in God's favour; and, in verses 7 and 9 of the same chapter, Judah is *subordinate* to Israel; while in chapter 3:18, it is clear that Israel and Judah are in separation prior to their return to Palestine. Thus we can see how necessary it is to interpret the prophetical books of the Old Testament in the simple literal meaning of its words. We have no Scriptural authority to do otherwise.

As regards the *perpetuity* of David's Throne, the Rev. F. R. A. Glover, in his work published some sixty years ago, *England, the Remnant of Judah and Israel of Ephraim*, remarks therein, "England is, in her Royal Family, of the stem of Jesse, and, therefore, is, as the hereditary holder of the perpetual sceptre and inheritor of the standard of Judah, the fostered remnant of Judah (*Jeremiah* 25:11;

Genesis 49:10)." When Israel and Judah return to their own land, viz., Judah "as a tribe," but Israel only *representatively* (*Ezekiel* 34:28; *Jeremiah* 3:14), they are to return together to that place from which they *together* came, many centuries since, under the care and leading of the Prophet Jeremiah.

The whole history of the Royal line of descent is ably described by Mr. Glover, who shows how Jeremiah, under Divine guidance, took charge of King Zedekiah's daughter, and safeguarded her to Ireland, where she wedded King Heremon of Tara, and thus preserved the direct line from David through the Kings of Ireland, and thence through the Kings of Scotland and England down to George V. Thus the Princess was enabled to reach the "isles of the west," the place ordained of God for "the planting" of His people Israel, and so the throne which was to be an everlasting throne was continued, and ready for Israel to serve under in the fulfilment of prophecy.

The Rev. Mr. Glover points out that in this manner is England's monarch descended from King Zedekiah's daughter, and by virtue thereof is the legal representative of the House of David, bearing the perpetual sceptre of Judah. Hence, it is that the sons of England have therefore a right to assume that they in her are, not only the *representatives* of Ephraim, but in truth the grand reality of that power of Israel. The author adds: "It is nothing to us that other nations shall deny this; there stands the fact!"

THE ESCAPE OF ZEDEKIAH'S DAUGHTERS
AND THE THRONE OF DAVID

Although King Zedekiah was the *last* King of Judah, the Bible records the escape of the king's daughters, under the care of the Prophet Jeremiah, accompanied by the Scribe Baruch. In the Book of *Jeremiah* we are given a lesson for our guidance. First of all foretelling the move to a *strange land*: "a land which thou knowest not" (*Jeremiah* 15:4). Then we are given the account of Ishmael carrying away captive all the residue who were in Mizpah, "even king's daughters," and then, in chapter 43:6-7: "even men and women and children, and the king's daughters ... and Jeremiah the prophet, and Baruch the son of Neriah, so they came into the land of Egypt." There the Bible leaves the history, but there is nothing recorded of Jeremiah's death. As the prophet had a mission to fulfil God's appointed mission would not fail to be accomplished in some manner.

It was (we are told) by an act of disobedience that the royal household was taken away to Egypt. "So they came into the land of Egypt, for they obeyed not the voice of the Lord" (*Jeremiah* 43:7). They were commanded to leave: "For I will punish them that dwell in the land of Egypt"! They were commanded to go to the North and West to Tarshish: "And I will set a sign among them, and I will send those that escape of them, unto the Nations, to Tarshish, Pul and Lud, that draw the bow, to Tubal and Javan, *to the isles afar off,* they have not heard My fame, neither have seen My glory: and they shall declare My glory among the Gentiles" (*Isaiah* 66:19). "To Tarshish and to the Isles afar off!"

If we turn now to secular history, we read that in 585 BC, which would be just after Jeremiah's journey from Palestine to Egypt, an account of the arrival in Ireland of a great prophet, accompanied by a princess, and a man, Simon Brug (Baruch), is recorded in the ancient Irish MSS., still preserved in Dublin.

Thus, taking up the ancient Irish history—or legends—in conjunction with biblical history, which leaves Jeremiah as shown, it becomes a very significant story; because, with the assistance of the seafaring tribe of Dan, it was feasible for the royal party to have journeyed to Ireland. Then we have the story of the marriage of King Eochaid-Heremon to a royal princess from Egypt, and preserving the line of royal descent from Zedekiah to our present King. Zedekiah himself had been—with his sons—slain, leaving no male heirs, so the throne could be perpetuated through the female line, as no doubt it has been.

This possibly may be the interpretation of *Ezekiel* 17 of the riddle, in parable form, to Israel of a great eagle cropping off the highest branch of the cedar of Lebanon, "he cropped off the top of his young twigs." "Thus saith the Lord God, I will also take of the highest branch of the high cedar and will set it, I will crop off from the top of his young twigs a tender one, and will plant it upon an high mountain and eminent. ..."

Zedekiah's daughter would here represent the "tender one" cropped off from the royal house, and safeguarded by Divine will, to a place of safety (Ireland), to there preserve the throne of David, which was ordained to be an *"everlasting throne,"* never to be destroyed.

It was the mission of Jeremiah to rehabilitate the royal house: "See I have this day set thee over the nations, and over the kingdoms, to root out, and to pull down, to build, and to plant" (*Jeremiah* 1:10). This was not to be done in Jerusalem, for Jeremiah was removed from Judea to Egypt, so his mission was elsewhere. We learn from chapter 44 that a small number "shall escape." It was open to Jeremiah to take ship with the Danites—the ships of Dan traded in tin and other things. Thus in Ireland it was possible the seed of David could "take root," and "Ezekiel's riddle can be thus solved." The "tender twigs" were Zedekiah's daughters; one of the twigs was planted by the great waters in a land of traffic. (See *The Lost Ten Tribes* by Rev. Dr. J. Wild, of America).

The escaping may very likely be of Jeremiah and the king's daughters to Ireland. Dr. Wild goes on to relate how Jeremiah did plant and build a throne, a college, and a religion—Ezekiel prophesied there would be three overturnings of the throne: "I will overturn, overturn, overturn it, and it shall be no more until He comes whose right it is, and I will give it to Him." Turn to history, the throne was turned over three times, from Jerusalem to Ireland, from Ireland to Scotland, from—or through—Scotland to England. This throne can never be "turned over" again, for Jerusalem is now incorporated into the British Empire, as Dr. Wild, writing in 1880, predicted that, in fulfilment of scripture, *it must be!*

The throne, religion, and education, established by the prophet have ever kept together. It is a pity more men will not interpret the Bible by the rules of common sense. It is written literally—why not read it so?

Remember God never promised to find the Jews another country; Palestine is specially reserved for them, *under the protection of Israel*, when they shall dwell together and appoint one head over them; for the Israelites, according to *Jeremiah* 3:14 are only to return to Palestine *representatively*. There should be no mistake on this point.

God declares *Israel* to be "His inheritance," and "the people that He formed for Himself." And to be the most powerful and prolific people on the face of the earth, to be "as the sands of the sea," "as the stars of Heaven." "I have sworn unto David, thy seed will I establish for ever, and build up thy throne to *all* generations" (*Psalm* 89:3-4).

It is specially significant that the Old Testament does not record the death of Jeremiah, nor anything further after his escape from Judea to Egypt in charge of the king's daughters! "Oxonian," in his work *Israel's Wanderings* remarks: "one thing is certain, that the line of sovereigns descended from Eochaid and Tephi has continued to the present day, i.e., through the early Scots Kings to the present Royal House of Britain. In this way God's promise to perpetuate the sceptre of David's family would be fulfilled: "thus saith the Lord, David shall never want a man to sit upon the throne of the house of Israel." Between Zedekiah and Christ was an interval of 580 years. Where was the fulfilment of this prophecy during all that time if the Davidic succession over Israel did not go on consecutively from Zedekiah?

It would be difficult to believe that it is merely a "coincidence" that we have the Lion of Judah emblazoned with the young lions on our Royal Standard together with the Harp of David; or that our land should be designated "Great" Britain, or be nicknamed "John Bull."

Again, it is not at all likely that after God had guaranteed the safety of Jeremiah with his "Remnant" (*Jeremiah* 15:11, 14), that a sudden end should befall the party. But it points rather to God guiding the prophet to a new land. It is another case of the sudden closing of God's history of Jeremiah—just as God closed Israel's history.

Therefore where they disappear from Sacred History we may well follow them by Secular History, and by such means we trace both to the British Isles. Probably the Tomb of Tara if investigated will clear up much of what is now obscure. We may rest assured that Israel never became extinct, nor Jeremiah left to die in Egypt; for both had their missions to fulfil.

CHAPTER XXII

THE "KINGDOM OF GOD"

From the many and various Scriptural references of the "Kingdom of God," there must be *two* kingdoms: one on earth—representing Israel of old—one in Heaven. That is, if we read the Bible in its literal sense. God's plan is to rule the world *through* Israel, and "the Kingdom of Israel" represents the "Kingdom of God" *on earth.*

In I *Chronicles* 17 we read that God ordains "a place for My people Israel." "I will settle him in mine house, and in My Kingdom for ever, and his throne shall be established for ever more." And in chapter 28: "He hath chosen Solomon My Son to sit upon the throne *of the kingdom of the Lord over Israel.*" This is clearly a reference to an earthly kingdom: "The kingdom of Israel," which is referred to in I *Kings* 11:31: "I will rend *the kingdom* out of the hand of Solomon...." This is "The kingdom" which was taken from the Jews! This kingdom was never a Gentile possession. Again, "the kingdom which is" represents an earthly kingdom restricted to Israel. The kingdom which *is to come* is the kingdom open to all believers, and which kingdom of God, in Heaven, will absorb the earthly kingdom of Israel, over which Christ Himself will reign during the millennium. That is, *the kingdom* of God, which "flesh and blood cannot inherit" (I *Corinthians* 15:50), and of which "it is easier for a camel to go through the eye of a needle, than for a rich man to enter" (*Matthew* 19:24)—God's kingdom of Heaven! Thus we can reconcile the scriptures to mean that God has ordained "His chosen people Israel," who became "the chosen" when the kingdom was taken from the Jews, at the crucifixion of Christ, to rule over the earthly kingdom, "until He comes whose right it is" to reign over the whole earth. "Till they see the Son of man coming in His kingdom," i.e., to set up Christ's throne in the place of the last of earthly monarchies.

"Thenceforward, My kingdom is not of this world" (*John* 18:36). *That* is the "kingdom of Heaven," open to the penitent believers in Christ of all races.

Most of our teachers and theologians would have us believe that "the kingdom" on earth is Christ's church militant. But if an actual material kingdom existed in David's day which was not "the congregation and elders," why should we imagine that the *secular* arm of the Lord has become abolished?

We cannot accept the theory that "the kingdom" means "the church," for do we not read in *Matthew* 21:43, that the kingdom was taken from the Jews; and yet St Paul declares that to them are committed the oracles of God? The kingdom of God, spoken of by St Paul, is a sinless one, but when Christ appears at His second advent "the Son of man shall send forth His angels, and they shall gather out of His kingdom all things that offend, and them which do iniquity." So there is nothing inconsistent with scripture.

If we understand there are two distinct kingdoms referred to in the Bible, we can then see more clearly what is meant by the many different references, which otherwise do not seem "to square" themselves.

British-Israelites believe that Great Britain—as Israel—holds the sceptre of the kingdom over which Christ is to reign on earth, and which is the kingdom referred to in II *Samuel* 7. Also that it is the same kingdom and people who have had a hand in the destruction of the past monarchies to fulfil. "But it (the fifth) shall break in pieces and consume all these (four) kingdoms" (*Daniel* 2).

CHAPTER XXIII

TO THE CLERGY

The general practice of looking upon "Israel," i.e., other than the known and recognised Jews as being "The Church" is their form of "spiritualising" God's promises (which were of a purely material nature) to Abraham. This practice unfortunately is answerable for much of the present-day unbelief and criticism.

The Clergy do not tell us how it is possible for "The Church" to be Our Lord's "Battle Axe," by which Nations are to be broken; or how "the Church" can "possess the gate of his enemies." Nor what is their interpretation of this passage "gate of his enemy."

They do not even explain by what means "the Church" has, in their eyes, been changed into "a Nation and a company of Nations," which God says Israel the old Nation was to grow into in the "last days."

They fail to explain who—in their opinion—are the "ten servants" into whose keeping Christ committed His Kingdom on earth, saying "occupy until I come."

Possibly some help would be afforded if some who are in doubt would read a book entitled *The Destiny of the British Empire and the U.S.A.* written by the "The Roadbuilder" pointing out how during the Great War so many Chaplains failed to inspire "Tommy" with "Faith" in the Bible, because they were in doubt themselves and can see no *literal* Israel other than the Jews. How then can the Clergy satisfy themselves, or their congregations, who is, and where is, the Kingdom of God which, *after* it was taken from the Jews by Our Lord was given to a "Nation bringing forth the fruits thereof"?

How do they explain why God said that one of the seed of David was to rule until Christ's Second Advent, if in their eyes, there is *now* no reigning seed of David serving as a King of a living Nation of Israel?

Surely the Nations to whom God committed His Earthly Kingdom were the "ten servants" or the Ten Tribed House of Israel to whom He entrusted the Missionary Work of seeking the "lost sheep" (or the House of Israel), sent, centuries earlier, into Assyrian Captivity, and who were to spread the Gospel throughout the earth; not, *as Israel*, but under another name and language. The English-speaking races are actually doing the greater part of all this Missionary Work, probably to the extent of nearly eighty per cent of the world's missionaries.

It is quite possible that much confusion has arisen over all this by giving credit to "the Church" for this particular work, rather than giving credit to "the Nation" for sending forth *from the Church* missionaries to carry out Christ's Commands in spreading the Gospel.

Another wondrous error amongst our clergy, and shared by the Head of our Church, is in classing all as being either "Jews" or "Gentiles," and looking upon the Anglo-Saxon race as "Gentiles" because they are not Jews.

Rather would it seem that Jerusalem was *saved* from "Gentile" control in 1917, and not merely changed over from the control of the Gentile Turk to that of the "Gentile" British, for if Great Britain be Israel they cannot be a Gentile Nation.

Will our Clergy, and more especially the Leaders, and Shepherds, explain why Israel's new name was Isaac—and, "In Isaac shall thy seed be called" (*Genesis* 21:12), if it fails to teach us that Isaac's descendants became Saxons? i.e., Isaac's Sons, Saac-Sons, or Saxons?

Is it not likely that it is the failure to obey our Lord's Command to "Search the Scriptures" and carefully interpret them, which is answerable for all the "doubts" of God's *actual words* written in the Bible "for our learning" as *meaning what they express*. It is also perhaps answerable for the wish of *some* critics who would like to see the Bible re-written and revised, as they think would be more in keeping with some of the present-day teaching, and their own personal views? No, we must leave God's Word as it stands, and as it has been handed down. Our duty is to Search the Scriptures, and endeavour to interpret them aright. If we accept the phrases as meaning what they express it becomes evident that the Old Testament is God's own History of the Nation of Israel who was to be an *Everliving* (though Concealed) Nation, destined to become very great and powerful in the "last days." "The Kingdom," in fact, which was entrusted by the Master to His Ten "Servants" (i.e., Ten-Tribed House of Israel) to occupy until Christ's Second Advent,—Israel "My Servant"!—the Kingdom of Our Lord and Master, which was to be reigned over by one "of the seed of David," "until He comes whose right it is" to sit upon the earthly throne.

We are taught by the Prophet Isaiah, in chap. 49: "Listen O Isles (the British or Covenant Isles) unto Me, and hearken ye people from afar" (the people of the U.S.A. and our overseas Dominions). A certain sign to us of our identity. Then read the whole of this chapter and see how aptly it fits the Anglo-Saxons. Then, too, the references to "Tarshish," and its ships, all of which seems to be confirmed by *Isaiah* 66:19; surely these "Ships of Tarshish" are, and were, the Ships of Israel, and Britain. Read I *Kings* 10:22; II *Chronicles* 9:21 and *Ezekiel* 27:12, 25.

Let us remember that long before our Lord's time metal was shipped from the British Isles (of the West) to the East, thus proving that the British Isles must have been, in those early centuries, a manufacturing centre for other overseas countries. This seems to be fully confirmed by the ancient historians who wrote before, and after Christ's time on earth, and made references thereto.

Therefore this seems a strong "sign" for our guidance that Israel—apart from the Jews—called "My Servant," must exist as much to-day, as of old; must keep the Sabbath as only we and the U.S.A. "Nationally" keep it; must be invincible in war, must be "the greatest of Nations," must *now* have a King of the Royal seed of

David, must be the "light bearers" to the Heathens, must be God's "Kingdom" *on earth* which is foreordained to be ruled over in future by Christ Himself on this earth.

Where then is Israel? Israel—"the lost sheep"? None of these characteristics fit the Jews, so *must* fit Israel. Finally, will any Clergy, or others, answer (logically) the following queries, in addition to those referred to above?

1. Where is the "appointed place" in which God promised that He would "plant His people Israel" (II *Samuel* 7:10).

Note.—Most certainly the Jews have not been gathered into one place!

2. In what manner has the "Church" become the "Nation," and the "Company of Nations" into which Ephraim was to develop? (*Genesis* 48:19; *Ezekiel* 37:19-21.)

3. In what manner does the "Church" possess the "gate of his enemies"? (*Genesis* 22:17).

4. In what manner can the Church come into possession of the area of land from "the River in Egypt to the great River Euphrates"? Has any of it fallen to the Church?

5. Who are the "great people"? (*Genesis* 48:19).

6. Who are "the children that thou shalt have *after thou hast lost the other*"? (*Isaiah* 49:20). Has the Church lost any?

7. If so, can it be explained that by forsaking her Communion they have become lost, but have established themselves as a "great people." If so, where?

8. In what way can be explained why God, on His Oath, swore that Israel should exist *as a Nation,* as long as the Sun, Moon and Stars continue to shine, if they can find no Israel other than the Jews now? Most certainly the Jews are *not* a Nation and have no King.

9. Can anyone argue that "the Jews" have developed into a Nation "as numerous as the sand of the sea-shore" and the strongest of all Nations? Most decidedly No!

10. Where is the indestructible throne of David? (*Jeremiah* 33:17). And where is the perpetual Sceptre of Judah? (*Genesis* 49:10).

11. How will the "Two Families" be reunited? (*Jeremiah* 33:24). And how will they choose themselves "one Head"? (*Hosea* 1:10-11).

12. If the Jews be the *only* Israel which they can see, can it be logically proved from Holy Scripture that Almighty God *has* fulfilled his reiterated promises? And are the following passages fulfilled in the Jews? *Deuteronomy* 33:13-16 "of natural riches, mineral and agricultural"—of being a "Maritime people," as in *Numbers* 24:7; Psalm 89:25; or of "ruling over many Nations"? or of "being ruled over by none"? (*Deuteronomy* 15:6).

If those who teach that "Israel" was exiled into obscurity (or intermingled with the Jews) and became, as "a Nation," extinct in the centuries BC, can satisfactorily solve these questions, then naturally they "Knock the bottom out" of all British-Israel "Facts," as shown above, and convert them into "Fictions."

Until this can be done, and done beyond a shadow of a doubt, the "Facts" produced must hold the day.

No amount of arguing can "convince" a person, unless one can produce with it some sound reason. There are many who are anxious to cast doubts upon the inspiration of certain portions of the Bible. But when we begin to doubt, where are we to draw the line? Because, to man's mind, one passage seems to be contrary to nature, as we understand the laws of nature, it is not for us to reject it as being non-inspired; or we at once doubt God's might and power. The Almighty who has created us—and the universe, and all therein, and to whom nothing can be impossible, however much so it seems, to our small minds.

It is surely—argue as we may—more reasonable to believe that God intended us to interpret the expressions in His Holy Bible just as they are written, and given to us, rather than for us to go out of our way to believe the words *mean* something different.

Therefore it is the Church who—as our teachers—must bear the blame for any false or erroneous interpretation which the "Church" places upon God's plain literal statements as recorded in the Bible.

When we are clearly informed that God made definite promises to Israel that Joseph's descendants should have certain possessions (of a material nature) in the latter days, and there should be a reunion of the separated Twelve Tribes; it stands to reason that God means to confirm His promises in a *literal* manner, for He cannot lie, and He cannot fail. To change the literal *everlasting* Nation of Israel into "The Church" is as absurd as it is unreasonable, for it cannot be *proved* in any manner which can convince one from the Bible.

It is this unfortunate "Spiritualising" which is answerable for so much unbelief and criticism of to-day. God's promises to Israel, God's written history of Israel, and His fore-ordained future for Israel, all show, in the clearest manner, that God *forgave* the outcast sinning Israel of old, which He punished by exile into Assyrian captivity, and then bestowed His mercy upon the Nation which He intended to be a great power in the world's future history. The "Stone Kingdom" recorded by the Prophet Daniel.

If we examine the history, and the characteristics of the Anglo-Saxon people, we see how wonderfully they possess all that the Prophets foretold for Israel in the last days.

Let us each answer, where is the Joseph's nation referred to in *Genesis* 49?

All those who venture "to doubt" the words of Moses and the Prophets are venturing to argue against the direct preaching of Jesus Christ; who remarked: "They have Moses and the prophets, *let them hear them....* If they hear not Moses and the prophets, neither will they be persuaded though one rose from the dead." And again: "If ye believe not his (Moses) writings, how shall ye believe My words" (see *Luke* 16 and *John* 5:47).

If Christ believed Moses and the prophets, by what possible right—or authority—may man, in these days, reject the writings? By what right can man place his own interpretation upon the prophecies rather than faithfully accept Christ's?

We can hardly argue that we accept the words of Christ as regards His preaching; but we reject the writing of Moses and the prophets. Simply because we have an idea (which we cannot substantiate from the Bible) that "the Church" has become "Israel." We must have sufficient "faith" to believe that "with God all things are possible," and therefore all that the prophets have written are true and have their special lessons, certainly we cannot reject certain passages of Holy Scripture and accept others! So long as our Church Leaders admit that the Northern Kingdom of Israel has been cast off for ever and replaced by the Church: so long shall we—nay, *must* we—be faced with unbelief, and infidelity, for we cannot in this case see any visible proof of the prophetical writings being fulfilled as regards God's promises to Abraham, Isaac and Jacob.

But what upsets our Church leaders greatly is, What has become of Ephraim and Manasseh? And, how are the twelve tribes to come into possession of the land of their forefathers? That territorial area which is described as lying between "the river of Egypt and the great river Euphrates"? Most decidedly that area of land cannot be "spiritualised" into something other than what the Bible *repeatedly* says it is, viz., *land*, and, in a certain position of the earth's surface. Anyone who dares to argue otherwise is self-condemned without doubt. But what a mistake to "blindly" lead the majority who scarcely read, or understand the Old Testament. The time has arrived for this subject to be closely examined, and without prejudice.

We must be honest, and we must admit, that if we reject a living literal Israel, we cast a doubt upon all the promises of God to Abraham and his seed. We also disbelieve that the Jews have to reunite with the so-called "Ten Tribes exiled to Assyria" i.e., reunite in a literal manner.

Unless we throw over the Bible we can *only* believe that God has *not* cast away His People, and placed a Gentile people in their place for Christ came to *redeem Israel*, not to destroy.

As the Rev. L. G. A. Roberts teaches us: "When Judah rejected the Lord Jesus, Israel, *redeemed*, began to take up the work, so until Judah proved faithless, to them was committed the oracles of God (*Romans* 3:2) ... the time has come, and these promises to Israel should now be no more 'spiritualised,' but acknowledged to be fulfilled in the British and Anglo-Saxon race, who are the literal seed of Abraham."

When the Jews rejected Christ the tribe of Benjamin, who had, we are told, returned from captivity *with* the House of Judah, accepted the Messiah, and this tribe spread abroad the gospel to the dispersed tribes of Israel,—or, as they were called by our Lord, "The lost sheep of the House of Israel."

The words of Zacharias in *Luke* 1:68-75 should teach our Clergy a wonderful lesson for a true and literal nation of Israel, and these words ought to be impressed upon every church-goer; for, when read in conjunction with a nation Israel, under a changed name, and speaking a new language, it becomes manifestly clear that God's promises *have been* fulfilled to the letter, and so the passage is not meaningless.

"Blessed be the Lord God of Israel; for He hath visited and redeemed His people, and hath raised up an horn of salvation for us in the house of His servant David; as He spake by the mouth of His holy prophets, which have been since the world began: that we should be saved from our enemies and from the hands of all that hate us: to perform the mercy promised to our fathers and to remember His holy covenant; the oath which He swore to our father Abraham, that He would grant us, that we being delivered out of the hand of our enemies might serve Him without fear, in holiness and righteousness before Him all the days of our life."

By this we know that the nation Israel, redeemed by the death of

Christ, has been "kept by the power of God through faith unto salvation *ready to be revealed in the last time*" (I *Peter* 1:5).

The nation Israel, that "in times past" (i.e., when exiled) "were *not* a nation," but are *now* (forgiven) "the people of God." The nation of God. The nation which (once) had *not* obtained mercy "but *now* have obtained mercy" (I *Peter* 2), as is shown above. Does not all this marvellous "fulfilment" of scripture give our clergy a proof positive of the inspiration of the Bible, and an answer to those who dare to throw doubts upon the truth of the Bible?

Whereas, try how they may, can any of our Clergy *satisfactorily* prove that Almighty God has failed to keep His sworn oath?

True there are great "Spiritual" blessings to be yet bestowed upon us *when* we, as a nation, become fitted for them, but we must not mistake the material promises for the spiritual promises of Salvation. There is a great distinction which is apparent to us when we accept God's word as meaning just what it expresses. The meaning of all this surely is, that God has selected His nation Israel to exist in order to form "His Kingdom," over which Christ is to come and rule on this earth during the Millennium.

It is an interesting fact, perhaps especially to the Clergy, that we are given so many passages in the New Testament which confirm the writings of the Prophets regarding what can only be *a Divine imposed "blindness" for a certain period of time in order to conceal Israel the living nation*, so as to live unrecognised through the ages.

Let us study a few, such as *Isaiah* 6:9-10: "Hear ye indeed, but understand not"; and again, see *Isaiah* 29:10-14 referring to the Lord "closing" the eyes, and "hiding the understanding of the wise." These writings must be given as "Signs" for our help and guidance: for we find St Matthew (13:14-15) refers to this "blindness," also St Luke (8:10), also St John (12:40), also St Paul (*Romans* 11:8), &c.

They certainly are no chance or random references by the Apostles, but rather to teach us "that blindness in part is happened to Israel," but this blindness is to last only "*until the fulness of the*

Gentiles be come in."

So we are permitted to know, that when that "*fulness*" be *accomplished* Israel, the living nation, will stand revealed to the world by a gradual progress of time, and events, each prophesied event, being an added proof by which to open our eyes: reluctant and unwilling though many of us may be to have our eyes opened to Israel being anything but "The Church."

Let the Clergy rest assured that these remarks are made in no carping spirit, but solely in order to try to arrive at the Truth of the Scriptures, and to prove the inspiration of the Prophetical Books as is being visibly shown to us day by day in the world's events.

Let everyone remember God's words: "Thou (God) wilt perform the truth to Jacob, and the mercy to Abraham *which Thou hast sworn unto our fathers from the days of old*" (*Micah* 7:20).

The following passages of scripture appear to be symbolical of the journey of Israel from the time of their escape from Assyrian captivity, until the time comes for Israel to be revealed; indeed, as a guide to us, in these days, of the manner in which the great "everlasting nation" (the "Stone Kingdom") which was destined "never to be destroyed" was to exist *unrecognised* in the world. "And I will bring the blind by a way that they know not; I will lead them in paths that they have not known; will make darkness light before them, and crooked things straight. These things will I do unto them, and not forsake them. Hear, ye deaf: and look, ye blind, that ye may see. Who is blind, but My servant? or deaf, as My messenger that I sent? Who is blind as he that is perfect, but thou observest not; opening the ears, but he heareth not" (*Isaiah* 42:16, 18-20). Then again: "Bring forth the blind people that have eyes, and the deaf that have ears" (*Isaiah* 43:8).

Thus, Almighty God led His people from the wilderness, to the place appointed, through strange lands, and unknown paths, unto "a place of safety," the "isles of the west," or the British Isles. And done in such a manner that Israel has never been recognised. The fulfilment of scripture, *still of the future*, is "the recognition of Israel, and their promised *re-union* with the Jews." "Then shall the children of Judah, and the children of Israel be gathered together, and appoint themselves one head ..." (*Hosea* 1:11).

"In those days (now approaching) the house of Judah shall walk with (or 'to') the house of Israel, and they shall come together out of the land of the north, to the land that I have given for an inheritance unto your fathers" (*Jeremiah* 3:18). This is a promise that Israel *shall* become the possessors of the "Promised Land," which is now held by Great Britain. Where is Israel? Surely Israel is the "kingdom" set up by God Himself, which shall never be destroyed? Such kingdom cannot be, as so many imagine it to be—Christ, because it is Christ Who is to reign over it. Christ cannot be *the stone* that "smites the image," for that "stone" is the kingdom over which Christ will reign.

Then we shall see the confirmation of the following prophecy: "Therefore, thus saith the Lord God—now I will bring again the captivity of Jacob, and have mercy upon the whole house of Israel ... When I have brought them again from the people, and gathered them out of their enemies' lands ... Then shall they know that I am the Lord their God, which caused them to be led into captivity among the heathen; but, I have gathered them unto their own land and have left none of them anymore there. Neither will I hide My face any more from them, for I have poured out My spirit upon the house of Israel, saith the Lord God" (*Ezekiel* 39:25-29). We shall also see the fulfilment of the prophesied resurrection of the "dry bones" of *Ezekiel* 37 where Israel and Judah shall be made "one nation" and "one king shall be king to them all; and they shall be no more two nations ... and David My servant shall be king over them.... ." "For had ye believed Moses, ye would have believed Me, for he wrote of Me. But if ye believe not his writings, how shall ye believe My words?" (*John* 5:46-47). "For whatsoever things were written aforetime were written for our learning." "Jesus Christ was a minister of the circumcision for the truth of God, to *confirm the promises made unto the fathers*" (*Romans* 15:4-8). Can anything be more definite, or convincing, viewed in the light of modern-day events "fulfilling the prophecies" before our eyes.

Christ says: "The Scriptures must be fulfilled," and in His Sermon on the Mount, "I am not come to destroy, but to *fulfil*" i.e., to fulfil what the prophets have foretold.

So many people ask, why is it if Israel and the Anglo-Saxon race be identical do our Church leaders reject it?

May it be answered thus? How was it when the Disciples heard that Christ had risen, said, "the words seemed to them as idle tales," and they believed not? Lack of faith! For Christ Himself remarked:

"O fools and slow of heart to believe all that the prophets have spoken" (*Luke* 24:11, 15).

Those readers who have compared the passages quoted from the Bible must satisfy themselves whether there is yet a more clear proof in the Bible that after Israel's deportation 721 BC only an Israel in a spiritual sense is to be accepted by the world. "The Scriptures cannot be broken," hence it behoves all students to interpret aright. Is the straightforward history of Israel's "future," so clearly defined in the Old Testament, merely an allegory? If the answer is in the affirmative then it is difficult "to square" God's promises as being fulfilled. If, on the other hand, we read the history literally, and compare it with the English-speaking races of to-day, we see every promise either fulfilled, or in the last stages of being fulfilled. And thereby we prove the truth, and the inspiration of the Bible to the satisfaction of the infidel and the agnostic.

If we argue otherwise, how can we account for or explain, why the Apostles Paul, Peter and James wrote as they did, making definite references "to twelve tribes which are scattered abroad." These Apostles must have known whether there were, or were not, twelve tribes, or merely the Southern Kingdom of the Jews whom they lived among and knew! Or why did Our Lord remark: "These are the words which I spake unto you while I was yet with you that all things must be fulfilled which were written in the Law of Moses, and in the Prophets and in the Psalms concerning Me"?

It is very evident that if the Northern Kingdom of Israel *had* ceased to exist, or had become extinct, or mingled with the Jews as so many really believe; Christ's Words would convey *no meaning*, for in such an event the Scriptures could *not* be fulfilled, and so we argue God's Word *has failed.* The Scriptures *have* been broken! What a terrible lack of faith in the Holy Bible. If only to obtain a stronger and greater faith in the truth and inspiration of the Bible it is with studying the truth of the identity of Israel which is so clearly and abundantly supported from *Genesis* to *Revelation*.

Let each one who has read these notes, decide whether the Bible can be accepted as "God's Word," seeing that, "All Scripture is given by inspiration of God" (II *Timothy* 3:16) and that Christ's command was to "search the Scriptures," i.e., the Old Testament —or whether we are inclined to follow some of the "Higher Critics" in their effort to belittle the Prophetical writings or cast doubts upon their inspiration or parts thereof?

"The Scriptures cannot be broken"

(*John* 10:35)

The Writer is indebted to the following Authors:

The Origin of the English and *The Evolution of Israel* by Major B. de W. Weldon, MC.
   God and My Birthright by Dr. J. Llewellyn Thomas.
   British-Israel Truth A Handbook for Enquirers.

And especially to the Rev. L G. A. Roberts (late Commander RN) and the Rev. G. H. Lancaster, Vicar of St Stephen's, Bow.

C. A. Hadfield, Major-General
April 1926

REVIEWS OF FIRST EDITION

British-Israel, Facts Not Fancies by Major-General C. A. Hadfield

We are very glad to recommend this most useful booklet which the President of the British-Israel-World Federation has just written. It is intended to present the facts of British-Israelism in a very serviceable and practical way for the benefit of those who may be enquirers after the Truth, or who may not as yet be convinced. In fact, as the cover says, it is a rudimentary guide to students of the subject. The General starts by emphasising the distinction between Israel and Judah, and he then proceeds step by step to show the salient points which serve as the biblical and racial proofs of our Israelitish origin.

We would rejoice to see this book very widely circulated; everyone should "read, mark, learn, and inwardly digest" it, for it covers the ground very efficiently in the space of some 30 well printed pages with clearly defined chapters. The value of the book is enhanced by a preface which the Bishop of the Falkland Islands has written as a Foreword, and we may say in his words "I therefore commend this book to all, and I trust that the blessing of God may rest upon it."—*The Banner of Israel.*

All facts are carefully worked out. No fancies or imaginations are allowed to intrude into the simple text of the enquiry—Does Great Britain answer to the picture set before us in Holy Writ for Israel? Does she occupy the place of their ultimate goal as foretold there? Are these prophecies to be realised whilst Israel is in Separation from Judah? or, as some incorrectly assert, after our Lord's return? A splendid pamphlet to put into the hands of any student of God's Word. An excellent book for a Christmas present or otherwise."—*The Covenant People.*

This useful booklet contains a foreword by the Bishop of the Falkland Isles. The sub-title states that it is a rudimentary guide for students of the subject, and is most useful for those who desire to know the fundamental facts of this great Truth. It emphasises the distinction between Israel and Judah, which is a basic fact of British Israelism, and then proceeds to prove, step by step, our Israelitish origin. We hope this booklet will be wisely read and studied by those in doubt upon this subject. It contains 23 succinct chapters, and can be obtained from Mr. Herbert Garrison, 57, Barrowgate Road, Chiswick.—*The Church Family Newspaper.*

An excellent compendium of Identity facts, it is a pleasure to read a book so free from the crotchets and extravagances which so often disfigure and vitiate this subject.—J. G. Taylor, Editor of *The Banner of Israel.*

British-Israel, Facts Not Fancies. A Rudimentary Guide for Students of the Subject by Major-General C. A. Hadfield. The Rt. Rev. the Lord Bishop of the Falkland Islands in a splendid foreword commends the pamphlet to all. His introduction alone is worth more than the insignificant price of this carefully worked out study.—*The New Watchman*, Boston, U.S.A.

FURTHER READING

A Synopsis of the Migrations of Israel by W.E. Filmer

The Covenants of the Bible by Rev. R.G.F. Waddington

Daughters of Destiny by G.S. Lewis

The Stone of Destiny by F. Wallace Connon

What Happened to Judah? by G. Taylor

All books from Covenant Publishing